You Can Pray
As You Ought!

You Can Pray
As You Ought!

BY
ARNOLD PRATER

THOMAS NELSON PUBLISHERS
Nashville • New York

Fourth printing

Copyright © 1977 by Arnold Prater

All Scripture verses unless otherwise marked are taken from the Revised Standard Version of the Bible, copyrighted 1946, 1952, © 1971, 1973.

Verses marked KJV are from the King James Version.

Verses marked *Living Bible* are taken from *The Living Bible* (Wheaton, Illinois: Tyndale House Publishers, 1971) and are used by permission.

ISBN 0–8407–5631–3

This is for Gene and Wilma Frank, who taught us that whoever stays with Him at Calvary sees Him first on Easter morning.

Table of Contents

Foreword

PRAYER IS IMPORTANT. It may be *the* most important part of being a Christian. I know that. I know it because God tells me in the Bible and in my heart that it is so. I know it because the Lord Jesus Christ gave priority to prayer. I know it because the saints through the ages have told us it is so. I know it because at the heights and depths of my own life, prayer has been the refuge of my soul.

But I also know that prayer is perhaps the hardest thing for me. Preaching, counseling, planning—all these I find much easier than praying. And I know that many other Christians—to our mutual embarrassment and guilt—have found this to be so. Our humanness and self-centeredness so easily short-circuit prayer.

I am delighted to recommend this book because I need it! I need the practical, biblical, up-to-heaven and down-to-earth sharing which Arnold Prater has described. And I recommend it to you, hoping you will find yourself drawn to be a "pray-er" more than ever before.

In August 1727 the Moravian Brethren in Germany began a round-the-clock prayer meeting. Twenty-four men and twenty-four women covenanted to each pray an hour per day for world missions and the unity of Christians. For nearly a century that prayer meeting continued uninterrupted. When one died, another would replace him, and within a few years after it began John Wesley was converted and the seeds of the Methodist revival were sown. The Great Awakening broke out under Jonathan Edwards in the American colonies.

Think what might happen today, a quarter of a millenium later, if God sent us a revival of true prayer. What homes might be reunited . . . what social evils put away . . . what new waves of evangelization might reach the nearly three billion who are without Christ in our world!

So read this book—with expectancy, and with the prayer I pray anew having read it, "Lord, teach me to pray."

Leighton Ford
Charlotte, North Carolina

You Can Pray
As You Ought!

PART I
Praying As We Ought

"...for we do not know how to pray as we ought..."

Rom. 8:26

Chapter 1

Save Us From Riskless Rhetoric!

NOW AND THEN God bombs us in order to blow our minds with awareness and understanding! Some time ago he really dropped a blockbuster on me.

We had returned home from a meeting in which, with no prior notice, the person in charge had called on me for prayer. As we were seated in our kitchen having coffee and discussing the meeting, my wife Martha suddenly said, "Oh, I'd give anything if I could pray like you!"

My first reaction, being both male and human, was to swell a bit inwardly and think to myself what a charming and intelligent woman I had had the good sense to marry!

But afterwards I fell to thinking about that statement. What was she really saying? She was really saying, "If I could put words and phrases together like you, God's attention would be attracted, He'd be quicker to listen, and I'd be more apt to receive His full consideration."

Is God really influenced by "good pray-ers" more than by those who bumble and stumble along, unable to extemporize? Do some "have God's ear" but not others? Is God "talked into answering" by the persuasiveness of our prayers? And are our prayers "ineffective" because we do not know how to express what we really feel?

Your answers to these and similar questions are extremely important, for they reveal what you believe about prayer, and *what you believe about prayer reveals the kind of God in Whom you believe!*

If you believe that some people, because they verbalize their prayers so beautifully, have a "pull" or an "inside track" with God, then you believe in a God who plays favorites and answers prayer on the basis of the excellence of its presentation. If you are a shy, tongue-tied person who stutters and stammers in prayer, then you're just out of luck. Perhaps God will listen to you someday when He's not too busy!

I want to say it again, because this is basic to any understanding of prayer: what you believe about prayer reveals the kind of God in Whom you believe!

Everybody longs to know how to pray, and to pray as they ought. Everybody wants prayer in their behalf; as I travel across this great country of ours the one phrase people everywhere leave ringing as a farewell is "Pray for me!"

This yearning for communication with God is inherent within us all. Young or old, learned or unlearned, rich or poor—everybody deep down longs to know God. I was struck with the universal truth of this one night in a service in which we had a time of prayer at the altar after the preaching. I moved along the altar, praying with each person. The first person with whom I prayed was an eighty-year-old man with diabetes. The second was a retarded man who mumbled as saliva drooled from his mouth. The third was a beautiful young woman, a former Miss America! Here was the whole gamut of mankind, all reaching upward for the One Whose name is above every name!

Save Us From Riskless Rhetoric

His own disciples watched Him. All day long the sick dogged His every step, the crowds pressed in upon Him and His enemies were always nearby waiting for the word which would trip Him up. By evening, being human as we are human, He was completely drained.

The disciples watched Him go away, dragging Himself up a hillside to be alone with the Father. As he came back to them the lines were gone from His face, the radiance had returned, and the amazing flow of dynamic energy that was His coursed through His being again. When they saw it they said, "Teach us to pray!"

So who really knows how to pray? The last thing I want from these pages is to appear to be the one with all the answers. The only time I am really an expert is when I am praying the Lord's Prayer, for He taught us that and we know it is proper praying.

Therefore, all I am doing in these pages is sharing what God has been unfolding to me on my journey, and what I have learned from praying at thousands of sickbeds and looking down into empty graves all these years.

But back to the blockbuster!

After Martha hit me with the flattering remark that indicated her admiration for my ability to pray, I thought about it for days. Here is a deeply committed Christian woman who has come a thousand miles further than I in her Christian journey. Yet it is true that while she is a gracious and sparkling conversationalist, when it comes to public prayer she becomes, like so many people, very, very shy. And she would not mind my saying that she gets very uptight when she knows in advance she will be praying in public.

On the other hand, I have been a public speaker all my adult life and it is very easy for me to put words together. Sometimes it reminds me of the person who was late for a political rally only to find that his favorite candidate had

17

already spoken for thirty minutes. When he asked a by-stander, "What did he talk about?" the reply was, "I don't know—he didn't say!"

Do I really have an advantage over Martha in prayer? I puzzled over this for days before I realized it *was* literally a blockbuster, for it fragmented many of the impediments which were blocking my prayer life.

Most of God's blockbusters come right out of His Word. That's why we call the Bible the "living Word." That means God can lift verses, words, and phrases right out of two thousand, four thousand years ago and hurl them like flaming missiles down into the very midst of our cir-cumstances now, and crown them with relevance that be-comes our answer!

That's the way He did it for me. He gave me a very familiar verse, one which I had read many, many times before. I am very sure it has more than one meaning, but in my case it gave me a great liberty I had never had before in prayer and set me free to talk with God with a new boldness and power.

Here it is:

Likewise the Spirit helps us in our weakness; for we do not know how to pray as we ought, but the Spirit himself intercedes for us with sighs too deep for words (Rom. 8:26).

Read it in other translations and paraphrases; *The Amplified Bible, The New English Bible,* and *The Living Bible* are especially good here.

What does this verse say? It says to me that it does not matter whether or not you are glib of tongue. It doesn't matter if you can form beautiful phrases or sparkling sentences. Your techniques may be all wrong, your theol-ogy may be highly questionable, in fact you may be the "worst" pray-er you know, but it does not matter.

Thanks to the blessed Holy Spirit, everybody is *equal*

before God in prayer. The Spirit helps us in our weaknesses, in our improper understanding, and *conveys from our hearts to God's heart what is really there*, that which is impossible for us to put into words anyway! That is exciting to me!

The verse says that in the final analysis the *words* are not as important as the *heart*. The words are only for our convenience anyway. God doesn't need words; He didn't need them before the world was and He won't need them after the world is not. "Man looks on the outward appearance, but the Lord looks on the heart" (1 Sam. 16:7).

So when we pray, the Holy Spirit helps us and reveals to the mind and heart of God what we cannot reveal simply because we cannot put love into adequate words.

When this concept flooded my being and took hold of me, there was a rush of release such as I had never known. There was a new joy in prayer. Prayer cannot be a burden or a chore to me now, for I know God's ear is attuned to my heart and hears the real messages it is sending out, not the ones I used to frost over with the whipped cream of mere words.

So if words are not that important, and if the Holy Spirit communicates to God what lies in the heart underneath all our words, this also means we must be honest with God!

I heard Geraldine Conway pray one time "O God, make me a real person whether anybody's looking or not!" I believe that was an honest prayer. Once I heard the stingiest man in town pray on his sickbed for health. Is it honest to ask God to restore us to health so we can go on robbing Him of His tithe? Is it honest to ask God to heal us so we can go right on giving Him second or third place in our lives?

This verse says to me that God knows our hearts, and we are very plainly told not to deceive ourselves—God is not mocked! He *knows* what lies underneath our words.

O, I tell you it's great to be free and to know you can be

honest with God. For twenty years I got out of bed each morning, and more often than not in my first prayer time of the day I lied to God time after time.

I would arise and go to my quiet place; it was raining, I had a headache, the children were driving me batty, Martha had burnt the toast, the phone was ringing every five minutes, and I would begin my prayer in the same old way, using all the right words and phrases I thought would tickle God's ear and please Him and make Him proud of me. "Lord, I love You. Thank you for my family, thank you for Jesus, thank you for the church . . ." and on and on and on.

I guess the Holy Spirit just sat drumming His fingers on the table, interceding for me and saying "Lord, be patient. One day he'll wake up."

Well, that happened one day and I discovered I didn't *have* to lie to God. That precious verse told me He knew the truth behind my lies, so why not tell Him the truth?

Again, I am not setting myself up as an example, but only sharing from my heart what has helped me. Let me share what I might say to God in my morning prayer now on one of those horrible "burnt toast mornings":

Lord, You know how it is this morning. My feelings are in the way. I don't feel Your nearness—I don't feel as if You are within ten thousand miles of this place. Lord, I don't feel this morning as if You *are*, but I'm not trusting my feelings; I know how fickle they can be. They change with the barometer or when a virus comes, or when I have indigestion, so I'm not trusting *them*.

Lord, this morning I'm trusting Your *Word*. Your Word is not subject to the changing weather or to indigestion or viruses or circumstances; it just stands there enduring forever and changing not. *That* is what I'm trusting, and *You said* You would never fail me nor forsake me, and *You said* You would be with me always, and *You said* that when I come to You, You won't cast me out and that You'll be my strength, my salvation, and the light of my life. And I'm trusting in what *You said*. Nothing—burnt toast, headaches, rainy days—*nothing* is going to shake me loose from that!

And when I pray *honestly* like that, more often than not the feeling comes back. But whether it does or not, *He said* His Holy Spirit would intercede for me with sighs too deep for words (or feelings), and that will be good enough for me until the feeling *does* return.

Maybe you have never shouted in your life, but if that concept ever bombs your awareness just right you might shatter precedent and cause the neighbors to wonder just what happened over there! (In fact, I want to stop right now and say "Glory!")

Think of it! Wrong techniques, wrong words, questionable theology, improper grammar, stuttering—no matter! When we pray, the Holy Spirit comes swooping in and catches up the tremulous love and desires of our hearts and carries them in His precious arms straight to the heart of God.

The old song is right—"What a privilege to carry everything to God in prayer." Little children do not find it difficult at all to accept this concept at once, for they never doubt that God understands and has things under control.

A little girl was kneeling by her bedside saying her nightly prayers. Her mother passed along the hallway and looked in. She heard the little girl saying, "ABCDEFGHIJKLMNOPQRSTUVWXYZ." When she had finished, the mother said, "Darling, why did you do that?"

The little girl answered, "Well, there were so many things I wanted to say to God I just couldn't say them all, so I thought I'd just say the alphabet and God could put the words together."

Perfect. That's it!

Even though our words may not be very important when we are talking with God, they are most important when we are talking with other humans. There are times when the wrong word is tragic. Here again, we don't have to depend upon our own cleverness to think of the right words at the right time. I believe with all my heart that when we ask Him for the right words He gives them to us.

The same Holy Spirit who does not need words to carry our prayers to God can supply the words we need to say to another human. Promise after promise in the Bible assures us He will be our lips and will put the words into our mouths. And what a blessed comfort to believe this by faith. It really takes the pressure off and enables God to say what *He* wants to say to another human through us.

One of the most precious examples of this concerns a little boy I knew, four and one-half years old. He had leukemia, the quick-acting kind. He and his mother stopped by his father's office one day and the little lad was playing around the room. He climbed up in the lap of the fine young Christian secretary and said, "I won't be coming back here before long."

"Why not?" asked the secretary.

"Because I'm going to heaven," the little boy said. And Sarah Miller, strong in the Lord and with a quick flash of insight, squeezed him and in a matter-of-fact voice answered, "That's fine . . . tell Jesus hello for me, won't you?"

Right on target, Lord!

When we can't say the right words to Him, the Holy Spirit takes care of it. When we need the right words for humans, He takes care of that, too!

How can we lose, with a deal like that?

Chapter 2
Try It—You'll Like It

WE TRY TO save time, but He came to save us.

Usually when we pray our tongues are hanging out because we are so far behind with other things. A woman said to me the other day, "The only thing holding me together is my hair spray!"

She was only half joking.

In our country we own 65 percent of the world's wealth and consume 90 percent of all the tranquilizing drugs manufactured in the world. We are an uptight people in a hurry—there's no doubt about that. Someone has said everybody in America hurries like they've been parked overtime for an hour and a half.

That is also the way many of us pray. We dash in, flop down, and start giving God dictation at the rate of 120 words per minute with gusts up to 180! "Lord, now here's what I want you to do about this problem of mine ... etc ... etc ..." In our behalf I will say we usually say "please."

I know this is nothing new, but we need right here to be strongly reminded that prayer is communicating *with* God. One person doing all the talking and the other doing all the listening is *not* communication—it's monologue. When one person talks, giving ideas, expressing desires, verbalizing gratitude, and the second person responds with his own ideas, desires, and wishes, this exchange is dialogue. There can be no *communication* without dialogue.

So prayer is interaction between you and God; it's not a one-way thing from you to God or from God to you. He certainly doesn't want you to do all the listening so He can do all the speaking. Neither does He want you to do all the speaking.

How can we pull this off? How can we make our praying a two-way happening? Don't take my word for it—let's go right back to the storehouse out of which God drops His blockbusters. This time it is to the psalmist that God is speaking:

Be still, and know that I am God. . . (Ps. 46:10).

I'd almost have to say that's the best piece of advice in the Bible on how to live with peace of mind: be still. Be still, simmer down, calm yourself, knock it off, take a deep breath, shut up!

If you only have one minute to pray, use thirty seconds of it to be still.

If there is any one thing we need to learn it is that, so let's try it right now. . . . Just lay this book down and try this little prayer-experiment in grace. We're going to pray for one minute and use thirty seconds to be still. Watch the second hand on your watch—you're going to be utterly amazed at how long thirty seconds is. You probably haven't been that quiet for thirty consecutive seconds in days. Ready? Pick up your watch . . . let us pray.

There, wasn't that amazing? The psalmist never had a watch with a second hand on it, but he knew a great truth. The Holy Spirit through the living Word is trying to drop that one into our hearts . . . "Be still. . . ."

Try It—You'll Like It

Why the need to be still?

For one thing, if we are not still before we pray we are apt to short-circuit our prayers. Not many of us know much about electricity, but most of us know what a short circuit is. Perhaps the two simple diagrams below will help.

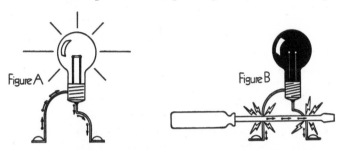

The diagram on the left (A) is an oversimplified picture of how electricity flows through a circuit properly; the result is that the bulb is lit. The diagram on the right (B) shows what happens when a metal object such as a screwdriver is laid across the two wires. The electrons traveling along the wire become confused. Some of them fall off, some leap forward, and some back up and are overwhelmed by oncoming electrons. As a result, a great surge of power backs up to the fuse box, blows the fuse, and the light goes out.

"Be still . . . and know . . ."

Now here on the left (C) is another simple diagram showing the proper circuit for prayer. There you are and you have a problem. The proper routine is to go to God. How? You are still. You are still until you become fully aware of Who it is with Whom you speak! Until this has fully permeated your mind and baptized it in a supreme realization, you are not ready to pray!

This is God! This is He Who in the beginning held in His hands the flaming mass and pounded out on the anvil of His divine will the earth, the planets, the stars, the galaxies, and the universe, and while He was at it, threw in a hundred million or so other galaxies and universes about which we now know.

This is God—that same God Who melted down all His goodness into the Lord Jesus Christ and became a baby born in a sleepy little town few people ever heard of! He bore upon His blessed shoulders all the sin of the world, and finally, because of what we are, He went down into death itself and came up on the other side and said, "I am the resurrection and the life . . . whoever lives and believes in me shall never die" (John 11:25).

This is that same mighty God Who is big enough to be everywhere and small enough to come and live in every heart; Who Himself is not so busy but that He takes note of the fall of even a little sparrow to the ground.

That is the God with Whom you are about to speak, and Who is about to speak with you. Thus, when we are still enough that we are aware of Him with Whom we propose to pray, we are ready then to pray! We are ready now to go along the circuit to our immediate life situation, our need, our problem. This kind of preparation keeps problems and circumstances cut down to their proper size; they never become bigger than God.

But most of us short-circuit our prayers. The diagram on the right (D) shows how we do this. We rush in, out of breath and in a hurry, panic-stricken with the possibilities that lie in our circumstances, and we begin to chatter. To God? No, not really. We bypass Him, and begin to pray to our *problem*. And it looms bigger, much bigger than God Himself. It is all out of perspective—a frightening, monstrous thing before which God seems really rather helpless.

So before we pray, we must be still until we *know* He is God. He is Lord. He is not only Alpha, but Omega as well.

Last fall I was on one of our great Missouri lakes on a fishing trip by myself. It was one of those perfect autumn days. The sky was God's most brilliant blue. The leaves were at their peak of color; they lay upon the hills like a many-colored quilt for some great giant from another planet. It was as if God's heralding angels had come through in the night, carelessly swinging their paint buckets across the celebrating countryside. The air was crisp and tingly and invited great deep gulps.

I sat on the far shore looking across the lake. There was not a hint of wind and the lake was a giant crystal mirror. The brilliant hills and the infinite blue sky were perfectly mirrored in the waters of the lake. And I thought, "That's how I should be before I begin to pray!"

Be still. How long? However long it takes, until the image of the infinite is reflected in my soul,* until the awareness of to Whom it is I am about to speak has baptized my consciousness. That is why before we pray we *must* be still.

I believe this is how we ought to pray. I am speaking, of course, of those times when we "go to our closets," when we go to "our place" to be alone with God. There are, of course other times to pray, but we'll let them wait a few pages.

Now at this point some have complained to me, "But I cannot be still; things dash into my mind unbidden. There is simply a parade of things crossing my mind constantly. How can I be still?"

First of all, to be still does not mean to have a blank mind in which nothing is happening. We are so made that this is an impossibility. The mind is never blank. Even in uncon-

*I am indebted to Dr. Lynn Radcliffe, who introduced me to this concept.

sciousness our minds are constantly active, as our dreams attest.

But what we *are* perfectly capable of doing is slowing it down, bidding it to perform at our command. So we slow it down, relaxing physically at the same time as best we know. I do not need to go into detail about that, for you already know some exercises of relaxation, I am sure. Here are a few devices I have found helpful in slowing down the mind to stillness.

Use the image-making processes as a device to prepare to meet God. Suppose I am in my "closet" or my quiet place, preparing to pray. My mind is feverish with the things of the moment and I am trying to create the proper circuit for prayer, first up to God and then down to my life situation. As I am trying to concentrate on Who it is with Whom I am about to speak, here comes this unbidden, distracting thought—a devilish little intruder. So I see my mind as a blackboard, and as the unwanted thought is written on the blackboard, I see my hand with an eraser in it and simply wipe the thought off and let God's face reappear.

Here's another. Using those same image-making processes, see yourself in a giant, clear capsule made out of love-plastic! This is my "serenity capsule." It is impenetrable. The only person who can enter it is the Holy Spirit. Though unbidden thoughts may come, they only smash themselves against the love-plastic surrounding me. Nothing can touch me. I am quietly anticipating the Presence. I am "kept safe in God our Father and in the Lord Jesus Christ" (2 Thess. 1:1, *Living Bible*).

Here's another. This one is great not only for the time of "being still" but also for all through the day. It is especially good for dealing with evil thoughts, doubts, fears, worry, and all the rest of the negative things from our unconscious minds which constantly rise up and gnaw and tear at us. I call these things "the voices."

Try It—You'll Like It

So when the voices begin, I see that negative thought as a little imp of the devil. To me he looks something like Reddy Kilowatt! But my imp has a giant key ring through his head. So I just lift him by that and slip the key ring over one arm of the cross of Jesus Christ. The blood covers him and he disintegrates! That's harsh, brutal treatment for devilish voices, but that is precisely what they deserve.

Let me suggest a few more little helpful "techniques" to help the Holy Spirit deal with the voices. See your negative thought as an ugly black spider sitting on a page of the open Bible, then slam it shut on him!

Psalm 84 says God is both a "sun" and a "shield" (v. 11). See your negative thought as a tiny weed with a brilliant ray of sunlight shining on it. Watch it curl up, catch fire, and disintegrate!

Have you ever seen a bird fly squarely into a plate glass window? God is a "shield," so hold up your shield, see the negative thought taking the form of a flying bird (better make it an unwanted starling!) and watch it fall as it hits.

Psalm 23 says goodness and mercy shall follow us all the days of our lives. Well, see "goodness" and "mercy" as God's German Shepherd dogs and watch them put your little imps to immediate flight!

Ridiculous? I want to suggest that these very down-to-earth methods of using our God-given image-making processes are not ridiculous. I'll tell you what is ridiculous: the forces of evil trying to make headway against a human being who walks through life with the Lord of all creation—that is what is ridiculous!

Even more ridiculous than that are the efforts of untold millions who do not know Him and who are trying to make it through life by their own talents, cleverness, and puny human wills.

Here's one more: when the voice begins, see it again as the little imp. Then take an appropriate verse of Scripture and see the print of the words strung out like a whip. Whip that little imp with it and watch him scurry away! I have several, but here's one of my favorites: ". . . be of good cheer, I have overcome the world" (John 16:33).

You can think of all sorts of devices to deal with these things which interfere with our quiet time, or which attack us at anytime.

Be still, and know that I am God. . . .

How hard it is for God to get our attention. That is why many times we should kneel to pray. Of course we don't do this to attract *God's* attention. We do it so He can have *ours*.

We are learning to pray as we ought, remembering always Rom. 8:26—". . . for we do not know how to pray as we ought, but the Spirit himself intercedes for us with sighs too deep for words."

You *can* pray as you ought, but you need to remember it is not these techniques, but rather the Spirit Himself who prays for us as we ought. Without Him the technique is nothing.

However, the technique is important to prepare our hearts, our deepest selves, so the Spirit can communicate them to God. We need the techniques because we are creatures of the five senses; we live in physical bodies in a world of matter, circumstances, situations, moods, schedules, calendars, and pains. All these tend to shut God out by their constant clamor for our attention, which is why we should not put down techniques designed to prepare hearts that are not phony or self-deceived.

Besides, when we are still we are waiting, and we have a clear-cut, definite word from God Himself about this. It is a real blockbuster.

They who wait for the Lord shall renew their strength, they shall mount up with wings like eagles, they shall run and not be weary, they shall walk and not faint (Isa. 40:31).

Try It—You'll Like It

Then too, it occurs to me that I never could have seen the image of the infinite blue sky and hills mirrored in the lake that October day had not the waters been still.

Try it—you'll like it!

Chapter 3

What Goes Up Won't Come Down

JESUS DIDN'T SAY you can prevent hurricanes, cyclones, floods, and tornados from happening, but He did say you can build your house on something that will stand.

Think of your prayer life as a house you are building. I promise that storms and floods will come and beat upon it, and the time will come when the house you have built will be the only place you have left for safety and refuge.

The universe is so set up that eventually the dilemma and the person come together. Every person eventually faces the position of personal helplessness. When that time comes, we surely need to have put up a house that won't come down.

We *can* pray as we ought; we know that now because we have God's promise. But we need a structure in which to house that blessed promise. We need some kind of pattern for proper praying.

So at this point I would like to offer a program for prayer. I challenge you to try it for a few weeks and then take a look at what has happened to your life.

I say again: I am not the final authority—this may not be

the best program of prayer there could possibly be for you. I may not even be *right*, but Rom. 8:26 assures me it is not necessary that I always be right, for it is the deep, unspoken intent of my heart which the Spirit latches onto.

In any event, I am simply sharing what has been helpful to me along the way. But since you are human and are traveling the same way, surely these things will strike some of the right vibrations.

All of us are constantly searching for new insights, but God won't give them to us until we begin to act upon the ones we already have. So let's get at it.

I would like to challenge you first of all to *a chunk of time in the morning*. Probably this will not be a big change for most. I daresay almost everyone who is the least bit serious about following Jesus Christ has already established this in their habit patterns—at least I hope they have.

A chunk of time in the morning. How long should it be? Well, I thank God that is one problem from which He has liberated me. I used to hear speakers talk about prayer; inevitably they would sonorously ask, "How much time did you spend with God this morning?"

As if God keeps books and gives us gold stars or brownie points for every hour we spend in prayer! If you know anything about grace, you know you do not have to collect brownie points with God. You don't have to woo God's favor; you don't have to reconcile Him to you. He has already reconciled you to Himself.

So how long should you pray in the morning? As long as you feel good about it! Sometimes that's five minutes (but if it is, remember to save two and one-half minutes to be still!), sometimes it may be twenty, sometimes it may be thirty. But if you are praying each morning simply to fill out a specified length of time, there are bound to come periods when you are really praying so you won't feel guilty about not praying long enough. Don't you think the Holy Spirit knows that?

What Goes Up Won't Go Down

Perhaps you will answer, "But I pray for thirty minutes each morning as a matter of self-discipline." If you pray in order to increase self-discipline, you pray for a different reason than I do. If you want to discipline yourself, then in my opinion you should jog, or do calisthenics, or work crossword puzzles. But I very definitely do not feel we little humans, mere specks of matter on the face of a hundred million universes, should use the Lord God of all *that* as a device upon which we can practice forcing ourselves to do something we do not really enjoy, but which we believe is good for us!

I can see the Holy Spirit drumming his fingers on the table again and saying, "Lord, this one is disciplining himself. His heart is really not in it. We'll just have to love him and wait—someday he'll be ready to pray."

Again I say: how can we truly pray until we are *honest* with God? Don't we know the Holy Spirit knows when our hearts are praying and when we are filling in time? So how long should that chunk of time be? Whatever makes you feel good and fulfilled, and again, since we are creatures of moods it will vary from day to day.

Personally, there are very few times I feel the need to pray for an hour. I just don't think it takes the Holy Spirit that long to communicate to God what's on my mind and in my heart.

Further, when we "set" a definite length of time which we seek to fulfill each morning, more often than not we grow inclined to say, if not verbally then at least by the way we live, "There now, that's *that*! See you later, Lord."

And finally, I never knew very many people who were long "pray-ers" who were not proud of it. I'd better not say any more about that . . .

So—a chunk of time in the morning. This period is the time for praise, petition, and intercession, or praying for others.

First of all, it's the time for *praise*. The Christian praises

God constantly, but morning is the time we *especially* praise God.

We can do that with the Psalms—they're great for praising God. Or if we wish to vary our praise we can just praise God by thanking Him. "Thank you, Lord, for another day of life!"

Do you know why you woke up this morning? It wasn't because you set your alarm clock or because you had enough sleep or anything like that at all. You woke up this morning by the grace of God!

It is not trite—it is truth to say that each of us is exactly one heartbeat away from eternity. In the unborn child the heart is about the size of a walnut, and it contracts and relaxes, beats for the very first time, and then continues on and on and on at the average rate of about seventy beats per minute for as long as eighty, ninety, or even a hundred years.

What causes it to beat? From where does the great heart muscle receive its commands? From the base of the brain there runs down into the thoracic or chest cavity a great nerve called the "vagus nerve." One of its branches goes to the heart and says, "contract, relax, contract, relax." This process goes faithfully on.

But what gives the message to the nerve? Well, they tell me there is a hormone-like substance in the bloodstream which constantly bathes the "ganglion," or nerve center, out of which the vagus nerve springs. As long as the ganglion is bathed with this substance, it sends out the signals. If it were possible to extract that hormone-like substance from the bloodstream and place it on the apothecary's scales, it would weigh one thirty-two-thousandth of an ounce.

Just that much right now between you and eternity.

So we really have something to praise God about, just for the mere privilege of waking up to a new day of life! Praise Him!

What Goes Up Won't Go Down

I knew a fellow who constantly praised God just for being born. Right on! If I hadn't been born, think what I would have missed. All the joy, the lessons of pain and suffering, the delights of a sunset, the fragrance of a rose, the smell of hot bread, the wedding kiss from my wife, the overwhelming glory of my conversion, my filling with the Spirit! Why, now that I think about those things and a thousand more I believe I'll just stop writing for a few minutes and have a glory feast to celebrate the great unspeakable blessing of just being born!

Morning is the time for praising God. It is also the time for *petition*.

Someone asked "Should we ask God for special things?" Someone else answered, "Yes, because if we don't ask for something special, what we'll get is nothing special."

Well, I doubt that, but seriously, a question is posed here. We have laid the foundation of our prayer-house on Rom. 8:26. So if words are not that important, and it is the unspoken desires and state of the heart which the Holy Spirit communicates to God for us, and further, if God knows what we need before we ask, why ask?

To ask God, to petition God, is not a contradiction of Rom. 8:26, in my opinion. If God is like a father, then surely we have a right to ask. We are invited specifically to "come boldly unto the throne of grace" (Heb. 4:16, KJV). Then, too, our Lord Jesus said, "If you then, who are evil, know how to give good gifts to your children, how much more will your Father who is in heaven give good things to those that ask him!" (Matt. 7:11).

When I was a boy, my father knew perfectly well that I wanted a bicycle. He knew it before I asked. He also knew whether or not I *needed* it. But I asked him for a bicycle anyway. He was not offended; he was my father and he loved me and it was my right and privilege to ask him. In this case he said no.

At that time I couldn't understand his reasoning. But

now I know something I didn't know then: my father loved me too much to give me a bicycle. South Washington Street in Neosho where we lived was the steepest street in town. It was unpaved and filled with deep chuck holes, great stones, and sharp flint rocks. If I had received a bicycle I would probably have broken my little eight-year-old neck before the sun set the first day.

So we do have the right of petition. But it is always within the context of Rom. 8:26. In speaking of this business of asking God, someone will surely quote part of James 4:2—". . . You do not have, because you do not ask." In quoting this they are implying that the way to "have" is to ask. But surely God is not petulant, holding back good things from us until we verbally approach Him about them. Is that the kind of God you believe in?

In my opinion it is not fair to cite James 4:2 unless the next verse is also quoted. This puts the entire thought into one sequence, without tearing it apart by a verse number separation. Now read the entire thought, James 4:2–3:

> . . . You do not have because you do not ask. You ask and do not receive, because you ask wrongly, to spend it on your passions.

This agrees perfectly with Rom. 8:26. The mere asking is not enough. The Holy Spirit will communicate to God *what lies in the heart*, and that will be at least one major factor in determining God's answer.

Certainly we should ask. A dear little turned-on Christian friend of mine is married to an executive who is moved rather frequently. Not long ago they were moved again, after having just gotten settled.

One of their friends was horrified to hear of the sudden, unexpected move and said, "Why, they have just bought that great big beautiful house!" Another friend replied, "Don't let that worry you—Nan will pray that house right into some buyer's hands!"

And she did!

What Goes Up Won't Go Down

Is God in the house-selling business? Again, you see there's no way to escape it: what you believe about prayer reveals the kind of God you believe in. My God is certainly in the house-selling business. He's also in the who-to-marry business and the where-to-go-to-school business and the what-shall-I-do-with-my-life business. If He has time to attend the funeral of a little sparrow, attend weddings, and hold little children on His lap, then I expect He would take time to sell a few houses along the way, especially since He might just happen to know some folks who desperately need just the right house.

I don't pretend to know why God helped Nan sell her house in a hurry, but Nan and I know she wasn't the slightest bit interested in exploiting anybody by making a big, unfair profit or "dumping it off" on someone. She just knew by faith that God had a plan for her life, and that in His marvelous wisdom and power, He would help her not only fulfill His plan for her and her family, but help some other folks at the same time.

So morning is the time for praise, and the time for petition. "Ask, and it will be given you. . . ." (Matt. 7:7) is the promise. Our God knows both our wants and our needs, and will answer in the most loving way possible.

Thirdly, your morning chunk of time is the time for intercession—praying for other people. Intercessory prayer is so big and so deep and so mystery-filled that we will devote the entire second part of this book to it. Even then, we will only be probing barely beneath the surface. But there could not be mystery unless there were answers somewhere, and while we will not dogmatically claim answers, we will be sharing some wonderful, thrilling things about this whole process of praying for others. It is so exciting and so spine-tingling I can hardly wait to get to it!

So let's just let it rest for now by saying that in building our prayer-house structure the morning chunk of time is for praise, petition, and intercession.

Now we will look at the second step in the prayer-house I am challenging you to build—a house built on rock, one that will stand against the hurricanes and tornados. This second step is *flash prayers throughout the day*. To many this is nothing new. Frank Laubach was master of this, but perhaps we'll have a new concept or two.

By "flash prayers" I mean little sentence prayers, hot from the heart, uttered throughout the day in every circumstance, at every hour, or perhaps in some circumstances every minute or so.

Over the sink, in the bedroom, in the supermarket, in the office, on the bus, waiting at airports, at the job—everywhere—shoot out these little fiery darts with which to quench the evil one and bring blessing to our little worlds.

What kind of flash prayers?

Some you will do regularly. I stayed a week in a home recently and had forgotten my lounging robe. A young college boy in the home loaned me his best red robe, and I enjoyed it so much that when I left he insisted I keep it. So I said "All right, I'll take it, and every time I put it on I'll say a prayer for you." Now many, many times when I reach in my closet for my red robe I say, "Dear Lord, bless Blake. Make his life really count for you!"

A dear lady in a Southern state had a problem. We counseled with her and when we left she gave us a tiny tree for our yard. When I see that tree I frequently shoot out a flash prayer for her.

These are *established* flash prayers you will want to say when you see articles of clothing, pictures of absent children, or whatever. To these you add *spontaneous* flash prayers. I heard a man cursing as he changed a tire the other day, and I sent a flash prayer on his behalf because he was letting his deep pain show.

If the Holy Spirit intercedes for us with sighs too deep for words, then when you have exhausted your prayer subjects for the moment you can simply whisper the name

What Goes Up Won't Go Down

"Jesus." And quick as a flash the Holy Spirit will transmit what is in your heart directly to God Almighty.

I don't know exactly how to deal with this theologically (thank God I don't have to), but I believe the name Jesus turns God on! That hot spring day when Jesus came up out of the muddy Jordan River after John had baptized him, God more or less said, "Now listen, all of you, that's My Son—and I'm proud of Him!"

If you introduce me to your children and say "This is Ben and this is Mary," I'd be interested, but truthfully, in a mild sort of way. But if you said, "These are my children—this is Ken and this is Judy," I'd say "Is that so? Well, those are the names of *our children*! Think of that!"

I'd get excited, and I believe God delights in that name which is above every name, and it just might be that the greatest prayer you prayed that entire day was when softly, out of the pool of love shimmering tremulously there in your heart depths, you whispered "Jesus, Jesus, Jesus."

So—flash prayers all day long. More about this in the next chapter. We know we cannot prevent the floods and winds and storms, but we are promised we can build our houses on something that will stand. But houses are more than fortresses against the storm; they are places where we live the abundant life every day. And that is perhaps a better reason for building a sound structure. The storms come only periodically, but daily living is a pretty constant thing.

We have challenged you to a chunk of time in the morning for praise, petition, and intercession. We have challenged you to the practice of shooting out flash prayers all through the day. Now for the roof on your house.

A chunk of time at night.

This chunk of time is for *balancing the books*. Perhaps you will do it before retiring, perhaps kneeling by your bedside, perhaps even after you have gotten into bed. But it is the time when you go back over the day. You thank God for every good thing that happened. You thank him for every opportunity you had to fill in some gaps where there was no love, or witness in some other way.

But since you haven't arrived anywhere near perfection yet, ask His forgiveness for the times you muffed the ball. You had an opportunity to help someone but you were too busy; you could have spoken a word of witness but you kept silence. You spoke when you should have listened, and perhaps a sharp, even angry retort slipped from your mouth in spite of everything. Just go over the entire day thanking God for the positive and asking His forgiveness for the sins committed.

There is no reason for Christians, who believe God accepts them just as they are and that Christ died for their sins, to wallow in prolonged periods of guilt. When Peter was an old, old man, that crusty old hyperthyroidic sword-swinger said, "Cast all your anxieties on him, for he cares about you" (1 Pet. 5:7), and if anyone had a right to know that, it was Peter!

Yet, of all the guilt-ridden people with whom I have counseled through the years, the most common complaint I have heard is this: "Yes, I know God has forgiven me, *but I cannot forgive myself.*"

Here is something hard to swallow. Whoever cannot forgive himself cannot do so because he still has within him a reservoir of self-pride. (Sorry about that, but you want it straight, don't you?) Whoever says he cannot forgive himself is really saying "How could a nice, respectable, good person like me have done a thing like that?"

Guilt is no good for anything after it produces repentance; all it is good for thenceforth is to wallow in.

So when balancing the books at night, you simply cast your burden on Him. I wish I could tell you all you have to do is say "Lord, I cast it all on You" and that will be the end of it. When you do that in your chunk of time at night, more often than not it is, but not always.

What Goes Up Won't Go Down

I must be honest enough to say that sometimes it takes months. When I was a very young person I once gave a message on "How To Forgive Your Enemies." Good topic, great need, everything fitted fine. I used the text ". . . Pray for them which despitefully use you . . ." (Matt. 5:44, KJV).

In effect, I told the people that all they had to do if they wished to forgive those who had wronged them was to get on their knees and pray for them, and God would just take the bitterness right out of their hearts.

On Monday morning, while I was still basking in the glory of all the accomplishments of the day before, the Holy Spirit (I can safely say it was He) said to me, "What about that fellow who cheated you out of seven hundred and fifty dollars?"

Then I remembered; it had happened a few years previously. I thought I had forgotten it. There was no excuse for the other fellow; as we say in the Ozarks, "He just flat done it!"

When it had happened my heart had filled with bitterness, resentment, and ill will. Time had abated the storm, but that Monday morning I peered to the depths of my soul and found a great pocket of poison still there. So I thought "Well, I had better start practicing what I preached yesterday." I got down on my knees and prayed for him, but when I arose I discovered that truthfully I still could hardly stand the thought of him.

So I thought, "Something is wrong here. I'd better keep after this." And I prayed for that dear fellow for at least six months. One morning I looked way down in the depths of my soul where life matters most, and I found that every last bit of this poison had been scoured out and cleansed by the persistent application of the fire of God's loving Spirit. All I could feel for this fellow was a deep, deep compassion and a great sense of sorrow that a human being, made in the image of God, would sell his soul for seven hundred and fifty dollars.

"This kind can come forth by nothing, but by prayer and fasting" (Mark 9:29, KJV), said the Lord Jesus. In this case I didn't fast, but I know now that resentment and ill will are the kind that go out only after much, much prayer. Otherwise, it lies deep in the unconscious, festering and boiling. One day it will come surging forth, externalizing itself in some great physical or spiritual symptom.

A man began a meeting once by saying, "Let us pray, and thus neutralize all the acids in this room." Isn't that great? It is also true.

So the evening chunk of time is for balancing the books. My chunk of time comes while I lie in bed. Some people have expressed guilt feelings to me because they have gone to sleep while praying. "Do you think God minds?" they ask.

Not my God.

My God is not a dignified old gentleman who is easily insulted by our weaknesses. My God is not "touchy" in His relationships with His children. My own children have gone to sleep in my arms as I talked to them. Is God less than I? Not hardly.

Finally, you can set your spiritual alarm clock by commanding your first waking thought, and it will generally obey. The unconscious mind is amoral, neither good nor bad; it is your servant. It only does what it is told and believes what it is fed. So boss it around a bit—tell it to awaken you with thoughts of love and praise and glory on your lips, and it will almost always obey.

Now back to your chunk of time in the morning, at your own "place" or "closet." Let me stress again the importance of beginning this period of time by traveling the proper route—first to God. Be still there until you *know* He is God. Then you are ready to speak to Him.

Here is another picture that may help us be still. Have you ever seen a ship go through the locks at the Panama

Canal or between two great lakes somewhere in this country? It is a sight to behold.

Picture a great ocean liner slowly coming into the locks of the Panama Canal. It encounters the lock and stops. The gates close behind it. It is enclosed in a concrete and steel alley. All its systems are shut down: the engines are stopped, the great propellers slow to a halt, the electrical system is shut off; the vacuum systems, the heating, cooling, everything stops and the great ship just waits.

Then slowly the gates are opened on the Pacific side towards which it is headed. The water begins to rise, so slowly you can scarcely see it with your eyes. Gradually the gates open and the water rises, and with all the great buoyancy and power of the ocean, that ship is lifted upwards and upwards. Finally the gates are completely open; the ship has reached the level of the Pacific, and *that* level, not the Atlantic level, is what is floating it.

Than all the systems are started once more: the great propellers turn, the lights come on, the power is there, and with the lifting strength of the Pacific mirrored under and about it, it is ready to sail out into the infinite of the vast ocean.

Be still. And when you *know* He is God, then you are ready to pray.

A chunk of time in the morning—the time for praise, petition, and intercession. Flash prayers throughout the day. Another chunk of time at night—a time for balancing the books.

So there you have it. A structure for a prayer-house that will stand. Begin building it today and you can pray as you ought. The Holy Spirit will see to that!

Chapter 4

God Is Your Best Friend

WE ARE ALWAYS more attracted to a personality than to an idea. Other things being equal, we respond more readily to a weak idea presented by a great personality than to a great idea presented by a weak personality.

I was attracted to the idea of marriage, but when I met the personality who could make the idea come true—wow!

Let's take the liberty of paraphrasing parts of the *logos* passage of the first chapter of John's Gospel.

> In the beginning was the Idea, and the Idea was with God, and the Idea was God. . . . and the Idea became flesh and dwelt among us, full of grace and truth; we have beheld his glory, glory as of the only Son from the Father.

A famous atomic scientist, in arguing before the United Nations for the exchange of students between nations, said the best way to export an idea is to wrap it up in a person.

That is what God did in Jesus Christ. He wrapped up all His love, His glory, His grace, His might, and everlasting purposes in a tiny little baby and deposited Him, born of a virgin girl, in Bethlehem's manger.

For one reason, among others, God did that in order to verify He is a *personal* God. You cannot pray to an idea, or a premise, or a concept. You cannot speak with a logical conclusion. We can only relate communicatively with other persons.

Later on, in the little book of First John, the author speaks of the One ". . . which we have heard, which we have seen with our eyes, which we have looked upon and touched with our hands . . ." (v. 1).

If some are "lukewarm" in their prayer life and commitment, perhaps it is because they are only committed to the narrative, the idea, the doctrine. But it was not a doctrine which died out there on that dirty little mountain shaped like a skull. It was not an idea they carried down the hill to a new grave and which burst the bonds of death. It was not a logical conclusion which came sweeping in like the wind at Pentecost to blow the roof off human despair.

It was not a set of facts that once came storming into my own life with love and forgiveness and transforming power, that turned me completely about and set my face in the direction of eternity. It was a real, live *Person*!

And if there is any one thing we *must* know it is that when we pray we are not praying to an abstraction but to a person. Our relationship throughout the day is with a living personality. If that is not so, then prayer is nothing but an exercise of self-delusion and mental gymnastics.

Someone has said, "Jesus came and put a face on God." Isn't that great? And it is true. You cannot say "God" and make any sense unless you first say "Jesus." Read that line again; it is all-important.

If you say "God" without first saying "Jesus" you get either one of two mental pictures. One is of a tired, bearded old man with a lantern and a staff walking around the creation and peering around corners at us. Or you might get the picture of a grey blob of ectoplasm swooshing from planet to planet taking care of things. Both pictures are eminently false.

But Jesus came and put a face on God, and as John said, "we beheld his glory." We can relate to a person, we can love a person, we can speak with a person, and listen to him.

When we hear the phrase "a personal relationship with Jesus Christ," that means we relate to Him not only as Lord and Savior, but also as a friend—one with whom we can communicate. That is what prayer is.

Precisely what does it mean to have a personal relationship with the Lord Jesus Christ?

All I can do here is tell you what it means to me. Let me start out by saying that everything we do is preceded by a mental picture of ourselves taking that action. If you wish to pick up a book, your muscles receive the signal from the nerves as a result of the mental picture you have of yourself picking up the book. It is lightning fast, that picture, but it is there. Every movement we make is preceded by these lightning-fast, subliminal, mental pictures.

We live and move about by what I have previously called the "image-making process." Everything we do is done by this method. It is the only way the brain has of triggering muscular commands. It takes place automatically—we do not have to make conscious pictures—but we *can* use this process to make conscious pictures. This is what we do when we daydream or fantasize.

We use the image-making process to commit fleshly sins—action sins. Every action is preceded by a mental picture. Sometimes I wonder why some shrewd lawyer has not used this fact to prove that there is, technically speaking, no such thing as "unpremeditated" crime. Perhaps he has—I don't know.

But this process is amoral. It is neither good nor bad. The use to which we put it is up to us. It is God-given, of course, or we wouldn't have it.

Therefore, if this is the vehicle we use to commit some sins, why could we who are so limited by these five senses of ours not use it with validity as a vehicle with which to glorify God and make a personal Savior more real to us?

I believe we can. What I am about to describe is certainly not original with me; many have used it through the ages. "Practicing the Presence" was the vocation of the saints.

But I live in the "now" and it was exciting and thrilling to me when I first discovered it, and it still is! Perhaps it will be to you. At any rate, my reason for dwelling at length on this in a book on prayer is simply because I do not see how we can pray with any effectiveness *to* Him unless we *know* Him!

We hear this great text time and time again. . . .

If my people who are called by my name humble themselves, *and pray and seek my face*, and turn from their wicked ways, then I will hear from heaven, and will forgive their sin and heal their land (2 Chron. 7:14, italics added).

The part I have italicized says to me something like this: "My people do not know Me; they wouldn't recognize Me if they saw Me. My people must therefore learn who I am *face to face*, and they do this by the method of prayer."

So in practicing His lovely presence we *look* at Him by the image-making process and then we really *see* Him with the eyes of the heart!

How then, do we practice His presence? Perhaps we can take our clue from little children. Jesus said that if we want to enter the kingdom we must receive Him as little children. Well, how does a little child receive Him?

When you listen to the prayers of your little children at night, what are they seeing? The power of the image-making process in children is fabulous. With it they can almost literally "see" what they wish to see. When your children pray at night *they see Jesus*.

God Is Your Best Friend

He is standing by their bedsides, His lovely face filled with tender compassion, yet behind that compassion there is veiled might and strength. He is tall, erect; His hair falls gracefully and naturally about His shoulders. His hand is outstretched over the bed. Your children speak to Him as naturally as they do to you. There is no guile, no affectation, no phoniness. To them it is real. When they have finished they go to sleep easily, quickly, and quietly—confident that the Good Shepherd will watch over them and keep them safe through the long night.

Does this say anything to us who are learning to pray? It should. But just then the scoffer will say, "Yes, that's lovely and sentimental, but it is not reality. The truth is that the little child uses that same image-making process to see such unreal things as fairies, goblins, and ghosts, so you cannot trust the faculty."

Yes, that is true, but it is only part of the truth. As that little child grows and matures, he will discard all those things he discovers are illusory and unreal as naturally as a tree sheds its leaves in autumn. But that which he finds is grounded in reality he will cling to the rest of his life. And it is the testimony of the church—the saints through the ages, as well as of millions of people now living—that the most thrilling reality ever to sink into a seeking heart is the empowering, thrilling, uplifting, loving presence of the living Lord Jesus Christ!

He lives! He lives! Christ Jesus lives today!

So we see Jesus, He who put a face on God. And we practice His presence all day long. When we come to our chunk of time in the morning and we are "still," trying to become completely aware of Whose presence it is we are coming into, we see Him. Each of us will have our own concept of His likeness. For some, He will appear in the likeness of their favorite painting. For others He will appear as a composite. Others will paint an original picture. But . . . there He is. How glorious—a personal God melted down into the likeness of a person. The smile is there; the love, yes; the firmness.

And there are the nailprints. The old song is right. *I shall know Him, I shall know Him, by the prints of the nails in His hands*. Then we see Him all the day long. In the kitchen, in town, at the mall, at the office—everywhere, He goes with us.

He goes on trips. I make many trips alone, and there was a time when I dreaded long drives or waiting in airports. But no longer, for I know His presence and I see Him seated beside me in the car, or on the plane. I see Him in hospitals. I would never enter a hospital room without pausing outside the door to say, "Please precede me, Lord Jesus, let this person see You and not me!" How many times have I gone into a hospital room and seen the face brighten and heard the words, "Oh, I'm so glad you've come!" Those dear ones, deep down, are not referring to me, not really, but to the One who is with me.

In meetings I have watched Him calm ruffled feelings. I have seen Him go about the room to bring it under the power and control of His Spirit.

As I meet people on the street it is my joy to say to Him, "Lord, bless that stranger and meet his needs. Enter into his thought right now and turn him towards You."

In the chunk of time at night He sits by my bedside, and in the morning when I awaken I look full into His lovely eyes.

I have been practicing His presence in this manner for about fourteen years now, but I want to insert a word of honesty here, and level with you. There are some days I am more successful at it than others. Some days I hit the ball out of the park. Some days I do just fair and some days I strike out completely! But I have hope because I am noticing lately that as I grow a bit along the way, the times when I muff the entire day are growing further and further apart!

God Is Your Best Friend

Continuing in this vein of honesty, there are some people who have less power to visualize than others. I spoke once to a group on practicing the presence and we used our closing prayer as an experiment for them to actually do it. Afterwards a woman came up to me with shining face and said, "All my life I have had a very poor imagination. I simply cannot see images; all I get is a grey blank. But when you asked us to close our eyes and see Jesus there came into my heart a great warmth and the greatest joy I have known in weeks!"

Let me make another thing perfectly clear. I know that the image I call up is *not* Jesus. It is an *image*, just that and nothing more. But it is a vehicle to help me make the presence of the living Lord whom I know by faith more real!

When I receive the Lord's Supper I do not believe for a moment that the juice and the wafer *are* the physical body and blood of our Lord Jesus Christ. But I do believe with all my heart that they are valid *vehicles* the Holy Spirit uses to make His wonderful presence more real. If you have never been deeply blessed in taking the Lord's Supper, then maybe you have never really taken it!

Therefore, intellectually I can accept the fact that the use of the image-making process to help make the presence more real is valid because it is the *God-given* process by which we live and move and have our very being.

If all this is only sheer mysticism and self-delusion, would to God everyone in the entire world were self-deluded. Most, if not all, the problems of mankind would disappear, and the kingdom of God would come quickly.

How can we pray to someone we do not know? How can we unburden the agonies and deepest needs of our hearts to a narrative in a book or a system of theology? The answer, of course, is that we cannot. We can only communicate with a person.

Let me here repeat: I am offering only what has been

most helpful to me. I am very sure it is not the only way, and may not even be the best way, but thanks be to God it doesn't have to be the best; it only has to be helpful for you and me. The Holy Spirit knows our hearts and we have the promise that He will communicate what is in our hearts to almighty God. What else matters?

I know this. No one can live on "Cloud Nine" all the time, or even most of the time. Life is set up so that we have to go down into the valley and wash underwear and dirty socks, pay rent, fix leaky faucets, mow the yard, sweep the rug, get bee stings, have colds, and wash dishes. No, we cannot be disciples of a man who died on a blood-stained cross and be "bubbly" all the time, but we can be *His* all the time—I know that for sure!

There was a time when I only sang these words, but I am so glad now that I can live by them:

And He walks with me and He talks with me,
and He tells me I am His own!

When we know Him face to face we can communicate, we can pray, we can listen, we can hear, we can see. That is what communication is, and it always takes place between persons who have a relationship that is for real!

But here is the best news of all. Anyone —*anyone*—can know Him in this way. He offers a personal relationship to all who will—that is the invitation. Little children, the elderly, the jungle savage, the secluded baron, the swinging socialite of the "jet set," politicians, ivory-tower professors—the word is "whosoever."

I certainly am not anti-intellectual; we are commanded as explicitly to love God with our minds as we are to love Him with our hearts. But I am so glad that formal education is not a prerequisite to knowing Jesus Christ, or to praying as we ought.

I wish you could have known my Grandmother Prater.

God Is Your Best Friend

She came from Kentucky to the southwest country in Missouri in a wagon. There on 120 acres of flint rock and brush she and Grandfather reared ten children. She was a pioneer woman in all the best traditional sense. She made her own soap in the back yard, washed clothes in a black iron kettle over a hickory fire, hoed corn, butchered hogs—she did it all. She lived to see six of those children return to the dust from whence they came.

She was up every morning long before daylight for forty years, and never baked less than thirty biscuits. She cooked, ironed, and scrubbed. The kitchen floor was made of white pine boards and they *shone* because she scrubbed them almost daily on her hands and knees. Her hands were always raw and red and cracked from the lye-water she used.

When she was old she grew stooped, and a great hump formed on her shoulders. Cataracts formed over both eyes, and seeing was difficult. Grandmother only had three months of formal education in her life. She started the first grade as a child but the term was cut short when funds were exhausted. Over the years she taught herself to read by reading aloud, pointing to each word and pronouncing it by syllables.

But she was radiant. She sang almost all the time. (I am sorry to say she had a terrible voice, but that did not matter and still she sang.) I can close my eyes and open my heart to those days of long ago, and still hear her singing as she went about her work:

> *My heavenly home is bright and fair,*
> *no pain nor death can enter there,*
> *Its glittering towers, the sun outshines,*
> *that heavenly mansion shall be mine!*

Again I can see her after the supper dishes were done and a dishcloth had been thrown over the syrup jar and the spoon holder. She would come into the living room carrying a coal-oil lamp. She would set the lamp on a table, settle down in her rocking chair, and take down the old family Bible. She would hold it close to her handicapped eyes and pointing to each word carefully, she would read aloud, "The—Lord—is—my—shep—herd. . . ."

I could have taken the theology of my grandmother and torn it to shreds. I could have told her about eschatology, sacerdotalism, bibliolatry, the apocalyptics of Revelation, the parallelism of the Psalms and the anthropomorphic theories of deity, and she wouldn't have had the slightest notion what I was talking about. I could have told her many things she didn't know about the man from Nazareth.

But she knew Him! And in the final analysis that is all that mattered. It's all that ever really matters. Anyone can know Him!

I do not know if I shall ever learn to pray properly, but I know I can pray as I ought. It is the promise of the Spirit, and I know Him. But better than that, He knows me! You too can pray as you ought. God has promised it, and it's been nailed down.

PART II
Praying for Others
As We Ought

."... the Spirit himself intercedes for us ..."

Rom. 8:26

Chapter 5

You Can't Get Fixed
Until You're Broken

THE FIRST TIME I sensed and recognized the power
of intercessory prayer was in Wheaton, Illinois. Billy
Graham and his party were having a crusade in the
stadium at Wheaton College. There were about eighteen
thousand people there, as I recall.

It was my privilege to be invited to sit on the speaker's platform that night. As I climbed the stairs to the platform, which was perhaps eight feet above ground, I
felt it. Of course, such a thing can never really be verbalized, but the nearest I can come is to say it was like
coming up from a cool basement into a warm house. There
was a definite "temperature change."

I sat there puzzled for a few moments as this great,
unseen outer warmth and power flooded in upon me.
Suddenly it occurred to me that across this world at that
very instant there were literally hundreds of thousands of
people praying for the man on the platform who was to
preach. Mr. Graham will be the first to tell you that prayer
power is the great single source of his continuing influence
in the world today.

Since then I have experienced this power several

times—the power of other people's prayers. I didn't say I could explain it; I only said I have experienced it. I had experienced it prior to that night, but I didn't know what it was until then.

Have you not experienced it in some great service of worship, or at the conclusion of some grand retreat, or in a dark valley of crisis?

Well, what is there about intercessory prayer? Do a hundred thousand people praying have more effect on God than one? Or a dozen? How many does it take to get Him to listen?

That brings us right back to the one persistent fact we cannot escape. What we believe about prayer reveals clearly the kind of God in Whom we believe. There's no way around it.

I do not believe God is overwhelmed by verbiage. Prayer does not "talk God into" answering; it does not change His mind; it does not suggest a course of action about which He had not thought. I have already made clear why I don't believe "the right words" in themselves guarantee an answer favorable to our requests. God does not have a supply of blank checks that He waits to hand out until He finds a person or group of persons who will press the button it takes to "turn Him on" to say yes.

But that is enough of the negatives; here are some positives. I believe there is far more mystery to "why" and "how" God answers prayer than *anybody* has ever even come close to knowing, but this does not mean we know *nothing* about it. We know some things because we have His Word.

There are two sentences in the Bible which, in my opinion, come nearest to describing the God as revealed by Jesus Christ than any other. One of them is in the Old Testament, one in the New.

The first is so obvious I need not say more about it. "God is love" (1 John 4:8). That says it all, doesn't it?

You Can't Get Fixed Until You're Broken

Here is the second:

The sacrifice acceptable to God is a broken spirit; *a broken and contrite heart, O God, thou wilt not despise* (Ps. 51:17, italics added).

There is something in God which responds to human brokenness. I cannot, of course, explain it except to say that in order to give us free will God gave us a spirit in which we were free to go our own way, covet His creation, and find the ultimate expression of that free spirit in rebellion by trying to kill Him!

Which is, of course, precisely what happened at Calvary. On the other hand, "The sacrifice acceptable to God is a broken spirit. . . ." That is, when we say to God of our own free choice, "Not my way but Thine," at that moment God is free to do that which by His own self-limitation He could not do until He found a spirit broken enough to allow Him to do what He wished all the time.

Further, nobody can say "Not my way but Thine" except out of a broken spirit. I don't want to get too heavy here, but we never know real truth unless we wrestle with it a while. So God, in giving us free choice, has said, "There are some things which by My own self-limitation I cannot do for them until they choose to let Me."

Now let's make sure you and I are communicating. Why did God limit Himself? Very simply because He could not grant *us* freedom to choose if *He* were free to interfere. Therefore in some things He *must* wait until our spirits are broken and given to Him. This seems to be a great secret of intercessory prayer, and I repeat it for emphasis: when God finds people who are broken enough to spend themselves in prayer for the sake of others, it releases Him to do what He couldn't do until He found those broken people.

I believe this is a valid conclusion because it is consistent with the way God operates in fulfilling His plan for our salvation.

Here was a lost world of unholy people; God loved them and wanted to save them. So our Lord Jesus Christ came and spent Himself completely upon Calvary's cross for their sakes. And when the Lord God beheld the brokenness of his own Son for our sakes, it freed Him to do what He could not, because of His holy nature, do until then.

"This is my body which is broken for you. . . ." (1 Cor. 11:24, KJV) was more than just conversation. It was the great key to our redemption.

Likewise in intercessory prayer, human brokenness is one key. When we are broken enough in spirit, when we care more about the beloved than about ourselves, it frees God to do what He could not do because of His own self-limitation until then.

This is in no way the complete and final answer to the mystery of intercessory prayer, but it has been helpful to me in trying to understand why we should pray for others.

Now let's go back to our morning chunk of time—the time for praise, petition, and intercession. Most of my petitions deal with the various situations which arise from day to day—strained relationships, new situations, spiritual problems. As these are answered and solved, new needs arise.

There are however, *some things* for which I ask Him constantly. One of them is for ears with which to hear the cries of people, such as the cry behind the seemingly routine phone call, or the mere "dropping in for a while." So many people all about us are crying out and we never hear beyond the surface chatter they put out. But the Spirit-filled person can hear things others never hear if he will ask God to give him ears to listen. So I constantly ask that I might hear people's cries.

Also, I ask almost daily that I might see people through Christ's eyes. Then I won't have to demand such perfect performance from them. If I see them through Christ's eyes, I will never see them as robot objects. The girl who brings my coffee at the restaurant will not be a mere waitress. The man who fixes my car will not be a mere mechanic. The person who waits on me at the store will not be a mere clerk. "Waitresses," "mechanics," and "clerks" do not hurt, bleed, and have deep needs. *People* do!

I want to see them as Christ sees them. Then I will not be distracted if they are old, or crippled, or retarded, or ugly; I will see them all as beautiful, desirable persons worthy, in God's opinion, of the death of His only Son! I will not be distracted by their shortcomings.

Another thing for which I ask God constantly is that His blessed Spirit will gently place His finger across my lips when the unlovely word or the hot reply arises to be spoken.

I have learned that my level of irritability is more apt to rise to the surface in the late afternoon and evening than in the morning. So in my morning chunk of time I always ask God to stay that unkind word or that cutting remark when evening comes. And I want to testify that more than once Martha has been spared my humanity because the blessed Spirit has done exactly what I asked Him to do. Further, I have not failed to thank Him. (When she reads this, I hope she won't, either!)

Remember, I am only sharing what has been helpful to me. Now for intercession. I have a prayer list. I hope you do too. Right now I am praying daily for sixty-two people. (If you admire me for this I will come back to haunt you! You can do it too, as you will see in a moment.) One is on drugs, another's children have strayed, some are lost from God, others are dying, and then there is our own family circle.

But how does one have time? And how does one keep from saying the same things over and over every day? That's a good question. I can't imagine anything more boring than saying the same things over and over, as if we have to give God an update and the latest bulletin concerning these people we love.

The answer? Right back to the cornerstone of this book, Rom. 8:26. The first lady on my prayer list is a woman we shall call "Alice." Alice is going blind, she has medical problems you wouldn't believe, and she has other problems equally as grave. The fact of the matter is she's in a mess!

But we love this dear lady very, very much. She is such a dear person that our very beings ache for her. We hurt for her in our own hearts.

So in my morning chunk of time I deeply believe that all I need to do is hold Alice up to God by name, pause, and perhaps with the image-making process see her for a moment in the arms of Jesus. And while I am thus pausing I believe with all my heart that the blessed Holy Spirit takes the needs of Alice in one hand and the human brokenness of my heart for her in the other and communicates them to God in ways far too deep for words or even for our understanding.

It is not so much our words the Spirit carries as it is our brokenness.

The sacrifice acceptable to God is a broken spirit; a broken and contrite heart, O God, thou wilt not despise.

It is no chore then to pray for sixty-two people daily—it does not even take much time. But what a joy it gives, and through the years at various times some marvelous things have happened in those lives that we know prayer has brought about.

I hope you have a prayer list. I'd love to be included in it. My list changes from time to time, but there are a few for whom I have prayed for as long as twenty years. What a joy to have prayer partners like that!

It is a blessed relief not to have to say to God every day,

You Can't Get Fixed Until You're Broken

"Now Lord, about that situation in Uncle John's life. You know he can't afford all that time in the hospital. You know his son needs to come home and see about him. Lord, please do something about that."

This would be acceptable for a while, but every day for six months, the same thing? How much better to claim the promise, and if *you* have done all you can for Uncle John, to just lift his name and wait for the Spirit to carry your hurt, love, and concern to the very throne of God! Always remember we are not seeking to free God to do what *we* want Him to do, but what *He* wants to do.

Now let's hurry on to some true-life examples.

Chapter 6

You Don't Persuade Him— You Permit Him

WHEN I WAS four years old I contracted a disease of the kidneys called nephritis. In those days they called it "Bright's Disease" in older people. To put it very simply, it was a complete stoppage of the kidneys.

My little body swelled to almost twice its normal size, and my temperature soared to astronomical heights. They didn't have antibiotics in those days or great bypass kidney machines which could wash and purify the blood. In fact, about the only medicine available was quinine, and I was given huge doses of it day after day. Sometimes I think I still can taste the bitterness in my mouth.

So the days passed until finally one night after supper the doctor came and he and Father went into my room. The doctor examined me and said to my preacher-father, "Jim, if there's anything you want to say or do for this boy, you'd better be doing it, for he won't be here in the morning!"

Father said, "Have you done all you know to do? Isn't there something else?" The kindly old doctor shook his white head sadly and said, "There's nothing more we can do, Jim, nothing!"

Father looked at the floor for a long moment, with the anguish in his heart that only a pronouncement like that could bring. Then he looked up and said, "Well, Doctor, there's something more *I* can do."

He turned and went down the hall into a bedroom where he fell to his knees at the side of a bed. Father *always* prayed on his knees, whether he was in the pulpit, at Rotary Club, or the PTA. It didn't matter where; it was his habit to pray on his knees. And that night he prayed something like this.

"O God, I don't have to tell You how dearly I love this boy, for You had a son once and You know. But dear God, I know You love him more than I, and Lord, if You want to take him then You can have him, for I know he'll be far better off with You in heaven than here. I just commit him into Your hands."

Then he went on, "But Lord, if in Your infinite mercy You spare his life, I promise to do everything humanly possible to see that his life is given to You in service Nevertheless, not my will but Thine be done."

When he had said that, almost in the next instant the doctor came, flung open the door and shouted, "Jim, come quickly, come quickly!"

Together they rushed into the room where I lay. The liquids were almost literally pouring from every pore in my body; the sheets and pajamas were drenched as the temperature broke and began to subside. In a few moments it was normal once more, and by morning the long road to strength and health had begun.

What happened? Did my father make a bargain with God? I don't think so. I don't believe in a God that small. Don't ask me to explain what happened theologically, for I cannot, and you would not respect me if I said I could. *My opinion* is that the complete relinquishment—my father's complete brokenness—was a factor, but that does not begin to answer *all* the questions which might justifiably be raised. Read on.

Little Michael (not his real name) was six and one-half years old—a precious, handsome little boy with a mind obviously on the side of brilliance. His parents are a young parsonage couple near us whom we number among our dearest friends.

One December day Martha and I sat in the waiting room in a hospital with Michael's parents waiting for the doctor's verdict. After what seemed an eternity the doctor came in and told us as kindly as possible that Michael had a terminal disease. His life expectancy at the very most was not more than eighteen months.

Then with the dammed-up frustration that all doctors who deal daily with such things must feel, he just stormed, "I don't know why it always seems to happen to the most promising and outstanding children!" Then, his difficult task accomplished, he wheeled and left.

A nurse led us into a room and closed the door, and of course everything in us broke up for a while at the news. When the first wave had passed we had a prayer together, and when I finished, Michael's father looked up at me out of eyes that were set free from anything life can do to a person and said, "Why Arnold, that doctor is wrong! Michael isn't going to die. Michael isn't going to die in a few months; Michael is going to live *forever!*"

Now when you can lay your faith up against a diagnosis like that and ten minutes later turn away in total victory, I say that's some kind of victory! That's the kind on which you can risk eternity!

The news spread throughout the area. Newspapers carried feature articles and churches formed prayer vigils until over the weeks there were literally hundreds of people pouring out earnest prayers for the healing of Michael's body.

We were close enough to his parents that we kept constant contact, and we knew the perfectly natural struggle they had at first in fitting all of this into their hearts. But shortly afterwards, one night at a great worship service, I knelt with them at the altar of God's church as they prayed the words, "Nevertheless, not our will but Thine be done!"

When they arose from their knees that night the complete victory over their circumstances was etched gloriously on their faces and in their hearts. From then on, Michael was God's problem, not theirs. I have never seen more complete relinquishment or personal victory over the inner self.

That victory continued right on down through the months of X-ray treatments, hospital stays, the whole bit. Never once did that peace which we can only call the kind that "passes all understanding" leave them. Never once was there even a flicker of anxiety. In all my ministry I have never seen serenity as complete and lasting as theirs. Little Michael's funeral was a veritable festival of joy, celebrating God's goodness, Michael's release, and the great sparkling truth that *nothing* can separate us from the love of God in Christ Jesus!

But now the questions come tumbling one after another. Why was my body healed but not Michael's? Was it because my father's faith was greater than that of Michael's parents? Was it because my father's relinquishment and brokenness was greater than theirs? Was it because my life showed more promise than that of Michael's? Was it simply because Michael's "time had come"?

If you say yes to any of those questions, you and I are on completely different wavelengths, and your God is different from mine. Those questions, in my opinion, are almost an insult to a loving God, but they must be asked and dealt with here, for across this world there are untold thousands of dear, deluded people who believe the answer to one or more of them is affirmative.

You Don't Persuade Him—You Permit Him

Let me deepen the mystery with another question. On that dark night long ago when my brokenhearted father was on his knees in that bedroom pouring out his heart to almighty God, so far as I know he was the only person in the world who was praying for me at that time. But in the case of Michael there were hundreds of praying people; no doubt many of them were deeply broken within and were offering the sacrifice of a broken spirit.

That raises some mighty questions about singular and corporate prayer. Further, sometimes it happens in the opposite manner; corporate prayer is answered in a manner we deem favorable, and individual prayer is not.

As if that were not complicated enough, let's muddy the waters a bit further. In a service of worship at which a famous woman faith-healer was presiding there was a man present with a very severe ailment of the shoulder. If he was a believer at all, he certainly was not "turned on." He did not believe in so-called "divine healing"; he went to the meeting to please his wife. Yet as he sat there in the meeting listening to the prayers, his shoulder was made whole.

So here is a case where there was *no* corporate prayer for this individual; neither (as far as we know) was there any one person praying for this particular man *at this time* (perhaps his wife, but we were not told of it).

So what about that? Mystery—deep, wide, unfathomable. I do not know the answers. All those are questions I'd like to ask our Lord further down the road.

What then? Are we to turn our backs upon all these mysteries and murmur piously, "Well, we'll just have to take them by faith?" Far be it from me to put down faith, but again we are to love God with our minds; to turn away from all this is simply to refuse to wrestle with these mysteries. I for one do not propose to do it, and I do not believe that is your desire either.

So although I don't have the final answers, I think it is perfectly valid to have an opinion, provided it is grounded in God's Word. In fact, does not faith always have its birthplace in an opinion? And in the Word?

From all this mystery I have drawn an opinion that has blossomed and matured until for me it has finally become bedrock belief and muscle-hardened faith, and that is *you cannot formularize God*!

God has not allowed us to become His puppets dangling at the end of a string, and neither will He dangle at the end of ours! More about this later on, but for now we can surely see we cannot wheedle a desired answer from God by backing Him into a corner and saying, "Now Lord, I've done one, two, and three, so You must do number four!"

I have been saying this for years and I'll say it again: if we do one, two, and three, God may do seven, or six and five-eighths. He will *always* respond with His will, and that may be right in line with what we had in mind or it may be 349 miles from what we thought He should do!

Now back to those deeply perplexing questions. Once more I do not have the final answers, but God has given me (and I have overtaken) a *concept* concerning them which satisfies me completely for the time being. It is a concept that gives me a fantastic advantage over my grandfather. His understanding could not possibly have been aided in this manner, for he was born too soon for this.

We live in an age of computers. No illustration is perfect (and neither are computers, as anyone with a charge card can probably testify!) but this one speaks to my soul's hunger. Though I know little about computers, I think I know the basic principles involved in their operation.

A computer cannot give an answer which has not been programmed (an electrical circuit established) into it. On television I watched a computer demonstrate how it could write the plot for a one-act play.

All the major characters in a play had been programmed into it—the hero, heroine, villain, supporting players, and minor parts. A given situation was fed into the computer and at once it began to write the play. Inside had been wired hundreds and hundreds of choices under certain given conditions and circumstances. So the computer went to work; it sorted through all the possibilities for that particular circumstance, typed out its choices and answers on that basis, and finally produced the finished script!

Marvelous! Wonderful! Fantastic!

Such complexity in a machine astounds me and starts my brain swimming with awe.

But wait! As we say in the Ozarks, "You ain't seen nothin' yet!" God Almighty is the Master Computer-Operator. He is perfectly aware of all the thoughts, instincts, ideas, desires, motives, earnestness, longings, personality traits, hereditary and environmental factors which are "programmed" into each of us. He knows every hair on our heads!

He also knows each individual set of circumstances in which each of us is living. And He knows in advance the *consequences* His answer to our prayers will have, not only for us and our immediate little circle of concern but among persons for perhaps generations to come. Just here it is time to insert Rom. 8:27. I love the way *The Living Bible* says it:

> . . . And the Father *who knows all hearts* [italics added] knows, of course, what the Spirit is saying as he pleads for us in harmony with God's own will.

So the Master Computer-Operator, Who knows all hearts and all the consequences of His answers not only in the now but for years to come, being a loving God, answers on the basis of His own will, which is always what is good and *best* not only for us but for many others who will be affected also.

This helps me with the unanswerable questions. It helps me understand why God sometimes says no or "not yet." It helps me understand why sometimes when there appear to be *no* answers and we are numbed by His seeming silence we must simply lean into the circumstances and trust Him!

But on what basis can we be asked to do a thing like that? Is it because when we run up against a blank wall we don't have anything else to say? Certainly not. I would not dare ask you as you hurt in the awful agony of despair to trust God if that request were simply all I could think of to say.

But I dare ask it because of the enormous certainty of the Word of God. Dear, dear friend, I have hardly been able to contain myself as I have waited all this time to tie this Word into all I have been saying up until now. You could not possibly believe that it is sheer coincidence that the next blockbuster is Rom. 8:28, could you?

> We know that in *everything* God works for good with those who love Him. . . .

That is why I dare ask you to trust God.

Brokenness and relinquishment release God, but not to perform as we desire; He is released to do what is ultimately good. And on the basis of His answers, no one will ever ultimately be cheated out of anything of eternal value!

So pray on! He is listening and waiting!

Chapter 7

You Want Miracles
Or You Want Your Way?

I AM ALWAYS amazed at what God does, but no longer am I surprised. If we cannot believe that in *everything* God is working together for good for those who love Him, then how can we really believe He is working in anything? To say that God has some select circumstances in which He chooses to work for good and that in some others He just simply "allows nature to take its course" is to believe in a smaller, less busy god than the God of all creation.

An answer to prayer becomes a "miracle" in our eyes when His work breaks out in such obvious fashion that we would have to be afflicted with acute spiritual myopia not to see and acknowledge it.

But He is working in *all* things. Whoever has watched a flower unfold, or seen a sunset, or heard children singing, or sat by a blazing fire has to believe this. Actually, a mockingbird singing at midnight or a puppy playing with a slipper is as big a miracle as the parting of the Red Sea. It is all a matter of relativity, and the miraculous is in the eye of the beholder, not in God's eye.

I am sure that is the reason we like to speak of physical healings in answer to prayer—especially intercessory prayer. That is great and it thrills us, but if we could really believe that the Master Computer-Operator is working for our good in *all things*, that would be the biggest miracle of all.

Still, God certainly is in the miracle business, and whoever puts down physical healings as second-class has never had one performed in behalf of himself or someone he loves.

So for right now let's discuss how to pray for miracles as we ought, for ourselves or for others.

I believe Danny Morris helped me at this point more than anyone else. In a great conference in the South I heard him tell how he and Dr. J. C. McPheeters were visiting an elderly friend down in Texas who was feeble and ill. When they were preparing to leave, the old fellow asked Dr. McPheeters to pray for his healing.

Dr. McPheeters said, "Very well; which one of God's five miracles of healing do you wish me to pray for?"

Surprised, the old fellow asked, "What do you mean?"

Then Dr. McPheeters listed the five miracles, one of which God always grants when we are praying for healing. Here they are as I remember Danny Morris recounting them.

1. Instant healing.
2. Normal healing.
3. He leads us to a remedy.
4. "My grace is sufficient. . . ."
5. He grants us a triumphant crossing.

Now let's take them one at a time. First of all *instant healing*. This is the miracle God grants least often. In the light of all the prayers for healing that arise to heaven it is rarely granted, but He does grant it. The story of my own recovery from nephritis is a graphic demonstration of this fact. The fever in my body did not gradually recede; it broke and receded instantly.

Practically everyone knows cases of instant healing. This

miracle is so obvious that it does not need much amplification by me. God grants the miracle of instant healing when it is in harmony with His will, when He is released to do so, and when on the basis of his Master Computer-Operator knowledge and on the basis of Rom. 8:28 it is what He chooses. There are probably many other factors involved in the mystery of "why" and "why not" about which we cannot possibly have knowledge as yet, but these are some factors of which we are certain, God being of the nature He is.

The second miracle of healing God grants is what Dr. McPheeters called *normal*. Of course all healing is normal for God, but by human norms we mean this kind of healing is the "automatic," uneventful kind.

For example, when you cut your finger opening a can, you usually hold it under the cold water faucet, run water over it, and daub a little antiseptic on it. You wrap it with an adhesive bandage and forget it. In a few days you remove the bandage and the cut has been healed. We think nothing about it because the body resources have taken care of it, and we *expect* it to be healed. In our minds there is very little question about it.

We do not regard it as a miracle, but even so it is as big a miracle as instant healing, because the Lord God performed both miracles. If God, through his creative masterfulness, had not constituted your body chemistry just as He did, the slightest cut would result in infection and death in a very short time.

That is why I said what I did about the Red Sea, and the puppy and the slipper. The unexpected is, to us, the miraculous, but if it is of God it is *all* miraculous. So "normal" healing is indeed miraculous, for most any doctor will tell you he himself does not do the actual healing—God does. Some of them will call it "nature," but that means "God" whether they use the right word or not.

The third miracle of healing God gives is that *He leads us to a remedy.* What a miracle this is! I know! Some time ago a sharp internist during a routine office physical examination picked up what he thought were signs of an abdominal aneurysm, a "ballooning" of the great aortic artery. Subsequent tests revealed him to be absolutely correct. I underwent surgery for it; the diseased artery was cut away and replaced with ten and one-half inches of Dacron artery.

It's working fine. I am as healthy as ever and restricted in no way except to a low-fat diet. My family doctor told me it was very unusual to discover something like this in an office examination (but then, the Holy Spirit could never be classified under the heading of "usual"). What would have happened had not the aneurysm been discovered and remedied? Well, in a few months the "ballooning" portion of the artery would have exploded, and that would have ended my tour of duty in this world!

Was it a miracle? If you were I you would believe it was. To me it is as great a miracle as if, after discovering the aneurysm, I had gathered twenty of my most faithful prayer partners about me and asked them to pray, and God had healed me instantly.

A remedy, whether it be medical or spiritual, has to be one of God's great miracles!

The fourth miracle God grants us is *"My grace is sufficient for you. . . ."* This is the miracle God granted Paul (although Paul had to ask Him three times before he got the message).

What a miracle it is to be given the grace to bear something you cannot bear . . . to withstand something you cannot stand . . . to carry a burden you cannot carry!

Sometimes I think this is God's most beautiful miracle: to see a human being under grace living with the impossible circumstance. Somewhere I heard the story of a man who was floating down the rushing river of life. He became stuck on a boulder, a huge boulder, a mountainous boulder, a problem that was unsolvable because the sheer force of the current kept him pinned against the boulder. He was trapped by his problem, with no way out.

So he cried out, "O God, help me or I'm undone!"

And the Inner Voice said to him softly, "My grace is sufficient for you."

The man railed at God, "Is that all You have to say to me? Here I am perishing and all You have to say is Your grace is sufficient. What does that mean to a man with a problem like this?"

The trapped man was baffled. He simply could not understand. So helplessly he just waited. Then, after a very long while, *the water began to rise*. Then he understood! Many times it is only after we float on up and out and away from those things which trap and block us that we get a clear look at God's grace, and celebrate the fact that indeed it is more than sufficient.

But what if the water does not rise? What if we do not float away from our problem? Well, of course, the answer is still that His grace is sufficient. I was pastor once of a woman who had the most severe, crippling kind of arthritis. One time she told me, "Sometimes the pain is so fierce that nothing can touch it."

I said, "What do you do then?"

She answered, "I get down on my hands and knees and pound the floor and say over and over again, 'His grace is sufficient for me.' "

Then with the kind of calm victory in her eyes that only shines from depths of conquered pain, she said, "And you know, Arnold . . . it always is!"

Can you believe that the grace to endure the unendurable might be the greatest miracle of all? Can you believe that sometimes He loves us enough to allow us to suffer? That's the kind of love that has teeth in it—no, that doesn't sound right: that's the kind of love with a cross in it! There, that's more like it!

That's all secondhand from others, but here's proof firsthand from my own heart. Fifteen days following the surgery to which I have referred, my ears began to ring—not softly, but loudly like the sound of an anvil after it has been struck. Naturally it was only a matter of hours until my already-weakened nerves were on the verge of shattering.

I went at once to a specialist. After a thorough examination he sadly told me he did not know the cause, but that it would not cause a hearing loss. It was probably due to circulatory changes in the brain, he said, and it might stop or I might have it the remainder of my life. There was no medical help whatsoever.

That night as I lay on my pillow, weakened, depressed, and contemplating the unbearable thought of having this horrible ringing the remainder of my life I fell to thinking of the Chinese water torture, in which the bound victim, lying on his back, has to wait as a drop of water falls onto his forehead at periodic intervals for days, until finally sanity leaves him.

I could see how this ringing could gradually bring about the complete collapse of my entire nervous system, and in the darkness I lifted my hands heavenward and cried aloud "O God, it's too much for me. I can't handle it. If there's anything to be done You'll have to do it!"

After a moment the inner voice came rising out of the depths we can never pinpoint or identify, and the Lord God of all creation whispered to one of His helpless, distraught creatures, *"My grace is sufficient for thee"*!

Then there descended upon me a blanket of serenity, peace, and inner assurance that made me know in the core of my being that it was all right! With the inflow of His grace, the boulder was behind me and I floated on down the stream. I turned over and went to sleep, and slept with peace. Once more I knew what the songwriter meant when he wrote "Safe in the Arms of Jesus."

You Want Miracles Or You Want Your Way?

That has been several years ago. Today I still have the ringing, but never *once* has there been the slightest dismay or panic. It is *His* problem and it can never touch me.

I know the Master Computer-Operator made the best choice for me in that instance, for now I can never be completely unaware of the flood of grace under which I am living. The ringing, though of course it would be pleasant if it were gone, sometimes becomes an anvil chorus of glory to the blessed Lord who really has overcome the world!

What a miracle!

The fifth miracle Dr. McPheeters mentioned was the miracle of *a triumphant crossing*.

I have seen people die apparently lost from God. I have seen them die under many, many circumstances. But to die triumphantly is a miraculous experience. No one knows how he will face death until he does it. So while I do not know for myself yet, I know He has the miracle of a triumphant crossing and that it is a definite answer to prayers for healing. No one will ever take blinded eyes, crippled limbs, accident-torn or cancer-eaten bodies with them into eternity. But to take a victorious spirit is perhaps the greatest miracle of all. It is a valid miracle for which to pray!

My own mother was granted this miracle. I have told of this in my little book *You Can Have Joy** but it bears repeating here. She was stricken with heart disease back in the depression days of the thirties. It was pretty gloomy about our house. My older brother lost his job and came home with two sick babies to live with us. My father received only a pittance of his salary, but it was Mother who kept us buoyed up.

She was radiant. She'd climb the stairs and stop on the first landing to catch her breath and clutch at her chest

*Marno Books, Route 2, Box 144-2, Joplin, Missouri 64801 (1971)

because of the angina. Then she'd go on up the stairs and soon we'd hear her singing:

> Sun of my soul, thou Saviour dear,
> It is not night if Thou art near,
> O may no earth-born cloud arise,
> To hide Thee from thy servant's eyes.

She knew she didn't have long. We'd go over to the church on Sunday and Father would preach about heaven. Soon the tears would be slipping down her cheeks and I'd think he was hurting her. I'd slip my arm about her to comfort her, but I know now that she didn't need any comfort. She was basking in comfort. She had so much comfort she didn't know what to do with it.

Finally the day came when she was breathing her last, and the family stood about as the great pains wracked her body. The last words she ever said were these: "Only a few minutes more . . . only a few minutes more!" and then she slipped away.

What did she mean?

Only a few minutes until all this physical pain would be ended? No, not at all. She meant only a few minutes more until she'd find the release she sought, and would enter into the other side where there is no pain, nor death, nor sorrow, and look upon the face of Jesus, her Lord, the Lord of Life. She could hardly wait. That's what she meant, and that is what I call a triumphant crossing . . . a miracle of God!

Danny Morris says that after Dr. McPheeters had explained this, he said, "Now, friend, which one of God's five miracles of healing shall we pray for?"

The tears welled up in the old fellow's eyes as he said, "Just pray that *His way will be my miracle*!"

That's it! Perfect. Right where it counts, old fellow. God will honor a prayer like that. But you cannot pray it off of the top of your head. It's got to be from the bottom of your heart!

PART III
Handling Prayer Problems As We Ought

"We know that in everything God works for good with those who love him . . ."

Rom. 8:28

Chapter 8

All Mysteries
Are Not Whodunits

SUPPOSE WE HAD God dissected and stretched out on the table of our understanding. Suppose we understood all things about Him within the limits of our finite minds. Even then there would still be a galaxy of unanswered questions and a hundred million "yes, buts. . . ."

I want to say again: God is not a concept!

This is where the Pharisees missed the boat. They chiseled Him out of the marble of their own conceptualizations. They wrapped up all their traditions and tied them with the string of finality, and they named the package "God." But when God came He couldn't zero in on them because they had jammed their own spiritual radar.

So even after you have finalized, summarized, and formularized Him, and have Him in your hands, He filters through your fingers like sand too fine to hold, and what you have left is divine mystery. That is because when you boil God down to the size of a concept He becomes a mini-God, for any concept of Him that will fit our minds is ultimately too small.

Does brokenness turn God on? Is there something about one human being broken for another which evokes a response from God and sets Him free to do what otherwise His own self-limitation forbade? Yes—but!

Yes, but there are countless instances when our human brokenness produces no *visible* or *comprehensible* responses. Does this mean sometimes God does *not* respond? We don't know, so here is where faith and knowledge end and mystery begins.

Is "faith" also a quality which when seen in human beings releases Him to do that which by His own self-limitation He could not otherwise do? It would *seem* so.

Over and over again Jesus lauded faith in others. Let's look at a few examples.

A ruler came to Jesus and told Him his daughter had just died. Jesus rose, and on the way a woman pressed forward and touched His garment. Jesus turned to her and said "Take heart, daughter, your faith has made you well" (Matt. 9:22). Another Gospel account tells of her complete brokenness and desperation, both factors we have previously noted. These plus her faith gained the answer she desired—instant healing.

A few verses later we are told of two blind men who cried out for mercy. Jesus asked if they believed He could do what they asked, and they replied "Yes, Lord." Then Jesus said a very strange thing, "According to your faith be it done to you" (Matt. 9:29). And their sight was restored.

Does this mean then that not only does it require faith to gain the answer we desire, but that the *amount* of faith we have is a factor? Yes—but—what about the man who went unwillingly to the healing service and who had *no* faith, and yet his shoulder was healed? The seventh chapter of Luke tells us of the young man Jesus resuscitated from the dead in a funeral procession, but the Lord asks the weeping mother *no* question about her faith.

On the other hand there is the centurion whose servant was paralyzed and in distress at home. This centurion told

All Mysteries Are Not Whodunits

Jesus it was not even necessary for the Lord to be present, but only to say the word and the servant would be made whole.

This evoked a tremendous response from Jesus and He said, "Not even in Israel have I found such faith (Matt. 7:10), and the servant was made whole.

This is the same Jesus who said that even a *small amount* of faith the size of a grain of mustard seed could move a mountain into the sea.

So in these incidents we find the following elements which seem to be present either singly or in groups in cases of prayers obviously answered: *brokenness, much faith, little faith, no faith.*

If you want to know the score you ask the scorekeeper, so let's dig just a bit further into the Bible and search for other elements present in recorded cases of obviously answered prayer.

Here is Jesus at the tomb of Lazarus, who has been dead four days. Jesus has traveled to the scene unhurriedly. Martha and Mary exhibited *strong faith*, for Martha said, "Lord, if you had been here, my brother would not have died. And even now I know that whatever you ask from God, God will give you" (John 11:21–22).

Then Jesus was moved so deeply that He shed tears, prayed, and called Lazarus forth from the tomb alive and well.

Now what we see in this incident aside from faith is the Lord's *compassion*. That is not the same as brokenness. They are first cousins, but not the same. Jesus cared so very much and it tore at His heart so strongly that tears of anguish flowed on behalf of the beloved.

In Gethsemane's dark garden underneath the olive trees the Lord Jesus had a will which had to be finally given to God. Here God was asking Him to shed His blood for the sins of the world and to begin a ministry of indwelling the heart of each person on the other side of the resurrection, wrestling with each person's will for possession of the soul.

He prayed, "Father, if thou art willing, remove this cup from me; nevertheless not my will, but thine, be done" (Luke 22:42). We do not know what else He said that night. We know that Luke says He "prayed more earnestly" (v. 44) and His sweat became like great drops of blood.

Here then is an element we have previously mentioned but which must be a great key, for it is given us in the example of our Savior: *complete relinquishment.*

Shortly after they were filled with the Spirit, Peter and John were going up to the temple to pray. (Prayer is what Spirit-filled people naturally do.) On their way they passed a man who had been lame from birth and who lay at the gate asking alms.

Peter fixed his eyes on the man and said to him, "I have no silver and gold, but I give you what I have; in the name of Jesus Christ of Nazareth, walk" (Acts 3:6). The man responded by "leaping up" (v. 8) and entering the temple with them to do a bit of praising and praying himself. (I should think he would!) So here is another element in obviously answered prayer, *the name.*

When Jesus came down from the Mount of Transfiguration He healed the boy with epilepsy. When the disciples asked why they could not do it He answered, "This kind can come forth by nothing, but by prayer and fasting" (Mark 9:29, KJV). Thus enters the element of *fasting.*

Enter now the church. Peter is in jail and they are praying for his release. An angel released Peter and he rushed to where services were being held and caused pandemonium. The church thought he was a ghost, that he'd been executed. They were astonished that God had answered their prayers. Here is one new element together with one previously mentioned—*little faith* and *corporate prayer.*

All Mysteries Are Not Whodunits

Then Peter was walking on the water towards the Lord when he panicked and began to sink, and cried "Lord, save me" (Matt. 14:30). It was the greatest prayer Peter (or anyone else) ever prayed. But the element here is *desperation*.

Listen to Paul and Silas in that Philippian jail. They had been beaten, kicked, cursed, and humiliated. Their backs are raw, their wounds still seep blood, and they are spread-eagled to the wall. But about midnight they begin to sing, pray, and praise God, and the walls of the jail fall down and they are delivered. So here is an obviously answered prayer in which there is the strong element of *praise*.

There are other elements found in obviously answered prayers recorded in the Bible, and you can search for them if you wish to pursue a fascinating study. But these few will serve to illustrate the point.

We should now naturally think that somewhere hidden among the elements of brokenness, much faith, little faith, compassion, complete relinquishment, the name, fasting, corporate prayer, desperation, praise, and all the other elements the Bible mentions, there should be a "key." And that if we found the right "key" or combinations of elements God would answer all our prayers according to our deepest desires.

But it doesn't quite come out that way, does it? Once the church prayed and Peter got out of jail. Paul sang, prayed, and praised God and got out of jail. Later on, however, they were imprisoned again; the church prayed, Peter and Paul sang and praised, but according to tradition they were both executed anyhow.

Why? Why did God let Paul and Silas out in Philippi but not later on? We don't really know. (Someone has said God would kick down the jail walls anywhere if it were the only way the jailer and his family could be saved!)

We know we cannot "program" God with the proper

elements so He will answer according to what *we think* are our best interests. He is the Master Computer-Operator and *He* does the programming.

If God is going to do as He pleases, then why pray? Please never ask that, for that question really means "If I am not going to get my way, why pray?"

There is much, much, much we can learn about prayer, and that is why we study and think and observe and listen. That is the reason for this book. Prayer is not a closed subject to a child of God; the Bible invites us, even urges us to "come boldly unto the throne of grace . . ." (Heb. 4:16, KJV).

But finally we have to face the reality that God is going to be God. We are not going to figure Him out, or bind Him to a formula, or capture Him in a box, or stake Him out on our leash. Sometimes He will do this and sometimes He will do that; sometimes He will speak, and sometimes He will keep silent. Sometimes He will overwhelm us with His seemingly eager response and sometimes in the *same* situation with the *same* set of circumstances *He* will leave us as He did Noah, day after day after day, sitting in puzzled silence.

Well, does all this mean we have an inconsistent God? One who is capricious, damanding faith at one time, not requiring it at another, Who answers to a small amount of faith sometimes and at other times only responds to a great display of it?

Again, what you believe lets us know what kind of a God you follow. To me, all this seeming confusion and contradiction is not that at all. It is simply a graphic display of the mighty mystery surrounding our loving God, mystery which is too deep for us ever to catalog, classify, cross-index, and file away under the heading "Mysteries Solved."

This does not mean we are not to love God with our minds. We should continue to do that if for no other reason than we are commanded by Him to do so. But before we ever start, we should know that this particular school which we are now attending does not offer graduate courses for which we are not ready. This life is only the warmup, anyway—eternity is the ball game!

Why am I saying all this? Because in our next chapter we are going to put the milk back into the refrigerator and bring out the meat. We want to back off and meet head-on some of the most persistently nagging and puzzling questions we know, questions I hear over and over again across this country. We would not dare plunge into a roaring stream like that without first admitting it is too much for us and that we will need the lifeguard before we ever get across!

But whoever has met the Lord in his own life does not fear the stream of mystery, for he knows the One Who made the stream! There are so many things *about* God I do not know. Just two days ago I met a retarded lad in church who wore a great big button which read JESUS CHANGED ME! I did not even smile condescendingly when I saw that; I prayed inwardly "Thank you, Lord, for doing just that."

And before these awesome mysteries you and I are that retarded lad and more. There are so many things we do not know *about* Him, this Savior of ours, *but we know Him*! And that makes the difference—Jesus changed me!

We know we can trust Rom. 8:26 and the blessed Spirit will communicate to God what we are not able to speak or even know! And that is good enough for us. And we know He is also the same God of Rom. 8:28, Who in all things is working together for our good. His answers are never on the basis of what is good for us but what is best.

That is why we do not fear to dig and scrape and plumb the depths of the unknowable because we know the One Who is knowable.

That is an answer as old as the book of Daniel. Remember Shadrach, Meshach, and Abednego? Nebuchadnezzar brought them to the great furnace out on the plain of Dura with the great golden image on one side and the white-hot furnace of fire on the other, and said in effect, "Now which will it be: will you bow down before the image I have made or will you be cast into the fire?"

They answered the king with these words:

> ... our God whom we serve is able to deliver us from the burning fiery furnace; and he will deliver us out of your hand, O king. *But if not* [italics added], be it known to you, O king, that we will not serve your gods or worship the golden image which you have set up (Dan. 3:17–18).

We know the One Who is knowable and have found Him to be trustworthy. Paraphrased simply, the answer of the Hebrew men was, "We know God can do what *we think is necessary*, but *even if He doesn't* (if He chooses some other way), we will still trust Him and be true!"

That is the Christian's answer in the midnight when the floods of bewilderment, confusion, and mystery sweep down over us.

Somewhere I heard the story of a man who had been a nominal disciple all his life. Somehow the vistas of his soul got stretched, and he came tremulously to the brink of a commitment in which he would turn his life completely over to the leading of God. This would mean that to wherever, whatever, and whenever God called, under His guidance the man's spirit would answer yes.

Gradually, as he drove home one night in the darkness, there came upon him terror as he thought of the things God might ask him to do. Then there came to him rising up out of those mysterious depths where God abides a voice which whispered this message into his ear: "My child, you can trust the man who died for you! If you cannot trust Him, who else can you trust?"

All Mysteries Are Not Whodunits

And that settled it all.

So it is with these great billowing mysteries. Why does God do this? Why doesn't God do that? Why does He answer thus here and so over there?

Even after we have earnestly and honestly struggled with these great mysteries we will end up panting—mentally, spiritually, and maybe even physically—for it is taxing. But out of it will come like Eden's mist falling gently upon our souls the blessed knowledge that even if we are mistaken in our conclusions, it will not defeat Him; even out of our wrongness He can work victory! His Word assures us of it. We know this because we know Him!

And besides, that man died for us!

Chapter 9

Dealing With Questions You Always Wanted to Ask

THERE WILL PROBABLY be more women in heaven than men!

At any rate, it would appear that way to me. As I go across this nation of ours from state to state and from community to community, women are constantly saying to me "Please pray for my husband. He doesn't know God!" Or "Please pray that my son will be saved!" Or "Please pray for my father!"

Very rarely do men ask prayers for the salvation of their wives or daughters. Seldom do children ask prayers for their sisters or mothers. All this leads us to the first of the great problems of prayer with which we want to deal (please notice I did not say "which we want to answer").

If God cannot violate free will, why pray for the salvation of another?

Even more mysterious than prayer itself is the human will and the freedom God has granted us with it. We have been saying that God has *voluntarily* placed limitations upon Himself. This means He cannot overpower and overwhelm us and say "You *will* accept my love and my

95

salvation." The human being can say "I will not" right on out into eternity.

It is easier for God to create a universe than to save one single soul! Think of that for a moment. Sounds incredible, doesn't it? But in creating a universe, God faces no opposition as far as we know. No galaxy ever says "no." No planet ever says, "Not yet." No sun or moon ever says, "Later on, perhaps, but not now." No cosmic nova ever says, 'When You give the life of Your only Son, I'll think about it."

I tell you, the freedom of the human will is an awesome thing! But do not be overawed by it, for even more awesome is the power of prayer! When we are praying for the salvation of another person we are actually engaging in spiritual warfare, a battle for that soul. We are girded about by the Word itself, for we are promised:

> . . . The prayer of a righteous man has great power in its effects (James 5:16).

When James speaks of "righteousness" here he is not speaking of human goodness. He is not saying that the prayers of a man who has an outstanding track record morally has great power. He is speaking of the righteousness of Christ. The prayers of a "saved" person, a person to whom the righteousness of Christ has been imputed, has "great power."

Well, specifically, what kind of power? For one thing, when you are praying out of a deep brokenness for the salvation of another, God is released to do some things He couldn't do until you cared enough to pray. I can imagine He might be enabled through His Holy Spirit to lead that person to the right place, the right time, or to another person who could help. I can imagine that God would be freed to bring conviction and holy pressure, the pressure of love, upon that person which he could not otherwise bring.

Dealing With Questions You Always Wanted To Ask

These are just a couple things one can think of which God might be freed to do in answering prayers for the salvation of others. We *know* this, that God wants to bring it to pass even more earnestly than we, and He has nail marks in His hands and a spear wound in His side to prove it!

It was suffering love that brought about our own salvation. When I finally yielded all my will to Christ and received Him as Savior, do I believe it was completely my own idea? Of course I don't! I know that my mother, father, friends, relatives, and others were deeply broken in spirit. Given the "right time" and the "right place," God was then able to break through into my awareness in a way He never could have were it not for the "great power" released by the prayers of those who love me.

Is God then more limited in seeking out a soul for whom there are none praying? For whom there are none broken? This may be the underlying yearning behind the cry Isaiah heard coming out of the anguish of God:

> And I heard the voice of the Lord saying, "Whom shall I send, and who will go for us?" . . . (Isa. 6:8).

He may be limited, but not defeated. And thus we come back and bow before the mystery, for we know God has ways, means, and resources we cannot know or understand. But in His divine hopes He is certainly aided by our prayers!

This should tell us enough to encourage us to pray on! Prayer does count! Love works! The sacrifice of a broken spirit is one that is valid with our God. We should never get the idea that God somehow is made prisoner of His own laws, for we are plainly told that *nothing* is impossible with Him. And if He will go to the lengths we saw on Calvary to try to melt us down, we know He will not turn His back, let up, get bored, give up, or be distracted. So pray on! And if the mystery of it all finally confuses and confounds you, pray on anyhow!

It needs, however, to be said that it is true that the possibility exists, as it must in the realm of true freedom, that that person may, of his own choice, finally close his own case, saying no . . . and therein lies the heartbreak of God.

But if I have a chance through the warfare of prayer to have a part in winning the battle for the soul of the beloved, then lead me quickly to the praying place, for I want to be about it! And if I truly love, then as long as I draw breath that one shall be the unceasing object of my earnest prayers.

When I pray should I say "Thee" and "Thou" or "You"?

This seems to bother quite a few people these days, but I am quite sure it doesn't matter one whit to God. It is not the words which the Holy Spirit communicates to God; it is that in the heart which is too deep for words.

But it *is* words that convey impressions of what it means to pray to the ears of listeners who might not know the Lord or who are newborn in the faith. When I was in the pastorate I was once pastor in a college town. College students were present every Sunday. All my life I had prayed in the language of "Thee" and "Thou" but the conviction came to me that the uncommitted young people in my congregation who studied Einstein, Von Braun, relativity, and space mathematics were not likely to be "turned on" by the 450-year-old language of Copernicus..

So I began to address God and to pray in everyday conversational language, both publicly and privately. It was terribly difficult, for I discovered it was a habit and I struggled with it for a year before I felt completely comfortable with my new style.

All this is not a plea for *you* to change—not at all; you should be led by the Spirit of God. I only recount this for the benefit of those who frequently pray in public, and they must be led of God and not by me.

Dealing With Questions You Always Wanted To Ask

Praying in the everyday language has helped me bring God from a difficult-to-approach level of loftiness to the level of loving, fatherly nearness.

But the final answer to this question, I believe, is that each person must be led in his own heart, and God will confirm your decision by the degree of comfort you feel in what you are doing—provided, of course you have consulted Him about it! If you have not asked Him about it, you might simply be comfortable in a familiar habit. But if you have asked Him, that should settle it for you!

How can I keep my mind from wandering?

I have never yet conducted a seminar on prayer but that this question is asked. It obviously springs out of guilt feelings, and this reveals that we believe in a God whose ego is ruffled if we don't give Him our undivided attention.

God, as we have noted, is not a dignified old gentleman sitting up in the sky just waiting for someone to offend Him! Besides, He is very patient. The truth of the old hymn "Just As I Am" applies to Christians, too.

However, in spite of this it annoys us to discover that our minds have wandered while we were praying and we have to yank our attention back on course. I am sorry to have to tell you, if you are a young person, that this flaw in our makeup doesn't get any better after one passes fifty!

So what to do about it?

A friend helped me with this years ago when he told me that the best preventive for this is to pray aloud. Verbalize the words.

Obviously, mind-wandering is not a problem in praying "flash" prayers; it occurs during our "chunks of time." So just pray aloud. One need not pray so it is audible to a person in the next room; all that is needed is simply to form the lips in a whisper that only we can hear.

This has not completely solved the problem for me, but

it has helped immeasureably, and I commend it to
you.

Should I always bow my head . . . close my eyes . . . kneel?

Again, habit enters the picture. We are comfortable in
our habits, uncomfortable in that which breaks the
routine. This is not necessarily a bad thing. We bow and
kneel because this is the basic approach we see characters
using in the Bible. We have been taught to do it and it is
second nature to us.

We bow our heads not only out of habit, but also because
we want to recognize that we reverence God. He is much;
we are little. The servant bows before the master for the
same reason.

God is our friend, our companion, the lover of our souls,
our heavenly Father. He is loving and warm and close, but
He is not our fellow-Rotarian or a back-slapping, hail-
fellow-well-met. He is *God*, and constant acknowledge-
ment of His lordship is a "must" for our reborn souls, for
their natural tendency is to usurp His creation and take
over His throne.

So reverence is a much-needed quality. We could learn
something from the Moslems in this matter. Do you realize
there is a reason they wear the "fez," the little brimless hat?
In the Far East, the sun is very, very bright. They wear the
brimless fez in order that their eyes may be forced down-
ward to avoid the glare of Allah's sun. They do not own
hats with brims.

So it is a good thing to bow one's head and close one's
eyes. We close our eyes to shut out the world with its
distractions, but of course we must finally say our posture
has nothing to do with our communication with God! The
Holy Spirit does not check to see if we have assumed the
prescribed position. Besides, if we are praying while driving down the freeway I wholeheartedly advise against closing the eyes!

Dealing With Questions You Always Wanted To Ask

The posture we assume is for the sake of our own hearts. This is also true in the matter of kneeling. We can certainly pray standing upright. We do not kneel to get God's attention, but so that He might have ours!

That haughty pride within us which often gives us our spiritual trouble is more likely to be subdued when we are kneeling and bowed down. It is pretty hard to be a big "I am" when one is kneeling before God—possible but not as easy!

If one is in an earthquake or a falling plane, if one is drowning or trapped in a burning building, or suffering a sudden severe heart attack, is God going to say, "Sorry, but you're not kneeling. Sorry, but your head is not bowed and your eyes aren't closed. Therefore you can have no audience with Me"? Ridiculous, of course.

Is it more than coincidence that when dealing with problems of praying we seem always to come back to the true state of the heart? That we always end up depending upon the Holy Spirit to intercede for us with sighs too deep for words—to communicate things to God which we cannot say?

I don't believe it is coincidence. I believe it is "God-incidence"!

Should I literally go into my closet to pray?

I do not mean to be flippant, but you would have a hard time in our house to find room in any of our closets in which to kneel and pray!

Let me hasten to say: I have literally done this, but I do not do it regularly. What I do regularly is to go to my *place* to pray. And I sincerely believe this is what Jesus meant.

The important thing is to put this command into context, so let's look at the entire passage:

And when you pray, you must not be like the hypocrites; for they love to stand and pray in the synagogues and at the street corners, that they may be seen by men. Truly, I say to you, they have received their reward. But when you pray, go into your room and shut the door and pray to your Father who is in secret; and your Father who sees in secret will reward you. (Matt. 6:5–6).

Now what is the subject of this passage, and the most important thing Jesus is trying to get across? It is "You must not be like the hypocrites." How must we do this? We must go into "our room." The meaning is "our special, secret place." It may be in our room with the door shut; it may be down in the barn; it may be out under a "special" oak tree—no matter. Wherever our *place* is—out of sight, out of the temptation to impress—that is where we should go.

My friend, Dr. Wallace Chappell, says he believes Jesus had a "place" to pray, that when Judas betrayed Him and led the soldiers to Gethsemane he had a good idea where he would find the Lord, for He had been there many times before. I believe this is a valid conclusion. Everybody ought to have a place.

A very dear friend of mine had a son who, like so many when they go away to college, was made giddy by his new-found freedom. He threw off all the traces, blasted out into the heady atmosphere of personal freedom, and started out on a campaign to undo everything his parents had taught him, to tear down every value they had instilled in him.

He drifted off into alcohol, pills, the whole bit. His grades went down and down, he lost interest in life, and his very person became a filthy thing. He stopped eating properly, he would not bathe, and his health deteriorated. He entered into long periods of depression and sat for long periods staring off into space.

Then something wonderful happened: he met the Lord Jesus Christ in a soul-shattering, head-on confrontation.

Christ just beat down all his stubborn rational lies, his proud ego, and his strictly intellectual approach, until by his own free will he came into the complete yielding of his life unto the lordship of Jesus Christ.

He came home to tell his parents about it and you can imagine the joyous celebration that followed. When they had dried their tears and sat down to talk about it, his father said, "Son, what happened? Your mother and I talked, we wrote and phoned, we did everything we could to reach you but nothing worked. So it couldn't have been us. Tell us, what happened?"

Then the happy lad said, "Yes, it was you, Dad, but you didn't know it. It wasn't anything you said; you never could have reached me that way."

Then he went on, "I was sitting in my room one night—heartsick, defeated, and desperate—and I thought of something. You didn't know it, Dad, but when I was in high school I used to come home late and I'd slip down the hall and you wouldn't hear me. But I had to pass your bedroom, Dad, and more than once I saw you in your pajamas, kneeling at your bedside praying for me.

"As I sat there in my room that night, with no reason for living and no hope for dying, suddenly in my mind I saw a picture of you kneeling there praying for me. I looked at my watch; it was eleven and I knew you were doing that just then. And Dad, that thought broke my last resistance, and I fell to my knees and cried out for God—and He came!"

God honored the "place" of that father and used it as a vehicle through which to reach a wayward son. Everybody ought to have a "place."

To whom shall I pray? Jesus, Father, or the Holy Spirit?

It does not matter, for we are not choosing between three Gods. The three are different personal manifestations of God. So we should pray using whatever name makes us feel at ease. Some people could not say, "Dear Holy Spirit" for the life of them, because of various reasons of word associations, and the same is true of "Dear Jesus." Most everybody can say with ease, "Dear God." I do not believe God minds what we call Him.

Personally, I am glad I am able to pray using any of the three names, but that does not mean I have an advantage over one who cannot.

So whatever difficulty we have in knowing what to call Him merely lies within us and not within God. Therefore, when we pray we should address God in whatever manner is most comfortable for us, always remembering He is more anxious to hear us than to be addressed "properly."

Should we praise God in prayer for everything that happens?

There is a school of thought just now which has as its basic tenet praising and thanking God for everything that happens both to us personally and in the circumstances which surround us. If you lose your job, praise God. If you break your leg, praise God.

I think I belong to the school just next door to this one, for I really believe that words have gotten in the way here. (They have a way of doing that.) I don't believe these folks really mean what it *sounds* as if they mean.

Here is one of the root Scriptures of this school:

> Rejoice always, pray constantly, give thanks in all circumstances; for this is the will of God in Christ Jesus for you (1 Thess. 5:16–18).

Remember once more that what we believe about prayer always reveals the kind of God we believe in. If you develop cancer in your body I do not believe you are instructed to get on your knees and thank God for the cancer.

Jesus plainly regarded sickness as part of the kingdom of evil, and He fought it with every resource at his command.

He said concerning the woman who had a "spirit of infirmity" and whom He healed on the Sabbath:

> . . . ought not this woman, being a daughter of Abraham whom Satan hath bound, lo, these eighteen years, be loosed from this bond on the sabbath day? (Luke 13:16, KJV).

If sickness then is a part of the kingdom of evil, and if Jesus fought it, I don't believe He expects us to praise God that it finally got a foothold in our bodies. But the Scripture is true and we ought to "give thanks in all circumstances." To me this simply means that if our bodies are invaded by cancer we should give thanks to God that *He is not defeated by it and for the victory He is going to work from it!*

We *can* give thanks to God in all circumstances, and it is His will that we do so! For it is God's business to turn defeat into victory! When you can walk up to the worst thing that can happen—the cross—and turn it into the best thing that ever happened, I say that's some kind of victory!

I once read a minister's sermon entitled "Thank God for My Heart Attack!" Intrigued by the title, I proceeded to read it. This man was not praising God that his coronary artery finally was blocked by a clot and the heart muscle severely damaged; he was praising God that the *instant* that evil thing befell him the Lord God began to work victory from within that circumstance.

He told of the stretching of the vistas of his soul, how his ability to empathize with his hospitalized members had been deepened, how he appreciated the great talent and skill given the doctors, how much more "alive" the love between him and his wife had become, what a sweetening of his sense of the nearness of God had taken place. On and on he listed the mighty victories God had worked from his heart attack.

So yes, we are to praise God always—not *for* the evil

things that befall us but in the *midst* of them. We can praise Him for the fact that He is not defeated and for the victory He will work from them! Pray on and praise on!

Why do we pray "through Jesus Christ our Lord"?

How often we read this in written prayers, or hear it in church, or perhaps close our own prayers this way. Why do we pray this way?

Well, of course by now we should know there is no "magic" in the words themselves; there is no "key" that unlocks affirmative answers. But still people have asked this question in our prayer seminars many times, so it is worth a brief discussion (notice again how we constantly steer away from the word "answer").

First of all we pray "through Jesus Christ our Lord" because He Himself said there is only one way to the Father and that is by Him (John 14:6).

I am a Christian. I have, by faith, accepted Jesus Christ as my Lord and Savior. But my performance is spotty, sinful, and imperfect.

Jesus Christ was God's own Son made man. *His* performance (obedience) on earth was perfect. God's holy nature demands that perfection. God has granted (imputed) Christ's performance to be mine, or in lieu of mine.

This means that when He looks at me, since by faith I have taken Christ as my Savior, God must see me *through Christ*. He sees Christ's obedience made mine. He does not see my stained, spotted soul. He remembers my sin "no more" (Jer. 31:34).

The reverse of this is also true. If I want to approach a holy and perfect God, I can only do it through a holy and perfect Christ Who has invited me to do just that. Therefore, when I come to God, I come "through Jesus Christ our Lord." He is the only way to the Father.

Secondly, I pray through Jesus Christ our Lord because, as we said in the beginning, it is the only way I can say

"God" and make sense. Jesus "put a face" on God; He gave God personhood. Since I can identify with personal love, I pray to God through Jesus.

But remember once more: these are truths for me to comprehend, meditate about, rejoice in, and be grateful for. They are not keys in prayer which make God listen. When I pray, I do not think of these great awesome facts each time, but the Holy Spirit remembers and communicates to the Father Himself my eternal amazement at God's love. Thank you, dear Lord, for an intercessor like that!

Is it all right to pray for the death of a suffering loved one?

Every time I hear this question it tears me up way down where I live, for I know it has arisen out of the agony of love in a heart-rending experience.

Here is a beloved father, perhaps ninety-seven years of age. His life is behind him and he longs for release into the other side, and someone asks me this question. If I say "Yes, it is all right," then you have the right to ask, "Then just where is the cut-off age? At what age do you cease praying for recovery and begin to pray for death? And besides, is it not a presumptuous thing for a human thus to usurp God's prerogative? Shall He who created life not retain the final right to its cessation? What does love have to say to this?"

I do not know the answer to this one; if I said I did, you would lay this book down and walk away, and you should.

When I was a pastor I prayed for the death of an individual only once. He was bedridden at home, elderly, and ravaged by a terminal disease. He was in what the doctor had only moments before told the family was the final coma.

As I held his hand in prayer before I left, I prayed that God would grant him the mercy of death, and release him from the body which was no longer of use to him. I went straight home, and in less than ten minutes his wife called and told me his soul had gone to the Lord. I bowed my head and thanked God.

Was I right in my prayer? I do not know. I only know when his wife called I felt a deep sense of peace and thanksgiving.

However, I did not rush right out and begin praying for the death of every "terminally ill" person I met from then on. For one thing, there are too many "terminally ill" people who have been physically healed and are alive and well today. I am one of them, as you have read.

I believe we cannot have a rule about this, but that our hearts should always be sensitive to God's leading from situation to situation, remembering that even if we pray mistakenly the Spirit will communicate to God the true intent of our hearts. Further, God will always answer on the basis of what is *best* for the loved one involved, no matter what kind of words we have used (Rom. 8:28 again).

If one of you who are reading these pages has prayed for the death of a loved one, and now you have second thoughts and guilty feelings about it, let me very tenderly assure you of a few things: (a) You did not pray God into something He didn't want to do. (b) If you did it out of love you did not commit a sin. (c) You did not "take the life" of your loved one. (d) God is not angry with you. (e) You did not deprive your loved one of the opportunity of getting well. (f) You did not change God's mind. (g) God will not hold it against you.

Should we claim a promise and "thank God it has been done"?

Over and over I am asked this question, for this represents a school of thought that insists God *always and only* answers our prayers on the basis of faith.

This school of thought says the way to gain the desired answers to our prayers is to ask God for what we want, claim the promise which applies, do not doubt for a moment, and begin at once the celebration that the desired result has been obtained.

This reasoning is most often applied when physical healing is desired, but it is also applied to other things—alcohol, drugs, money, and so on.

I remember being in a prayer meeting where a man came forward and laid a package of cigarettes on the altar. The leader laid his hands upon the man's head and prayed like this: "O Lord, You said in Your Word that if we ask anything in prayer, believing, it should be done. Now we ask that this man be delivered from cigarettes, and right now we claim the promise and we thank You and praise You that it has been done!"

He then shook the man's hand and together they praised God that the desired result had been brought to pass. However, in a few days I saw the man back at the same old habit.

Here is another extremely dramatic case of claiming that promise. A couple in their forties were childless. In their prayer group their friends gathered about and laid their hands upon the couple (I am not opposed to the laying on of hands; it is scriptural and I have practiced it), asked for a baby to be born of the woman, reminded God of His promise, and reminded Him of Sarah and what He did for her. Then they arose and celebrated the pregnancy. The couple marked the date of expectancy on their calendar, bought baby clothing, a bed, and made other preparations.

When sufficient time had passed it became obvious that nothing was going to happen. Their friends were too kind to say it to the disappointed couple, but the only explanation they could offer to one another for God's reluctance was that the couple "didn't have enough faith."

I could go on with some really strange examples of bald men who prayed for hair on the grounds that "with God nothing is impossible" and others who prayed for new teeth, actually discarding their false teeth in anticipation of the new ones God was going to grow.

Now lest some should think I am poking fun at these dear and very earnest people, let me give you another instance with which I am personally knowledgeable. A woman was hospitalized with a most painful disease involving the nerve endings in her skin. She could not bear the slightest touch of sheets, clothing, or hands upon her body. This, of course, rapidly eroded the tolerability level of her nervous system until she was on the very verge of complete nervous collapse.

Hospitalized, she had scarcely moved for days. One day the nurse was out of the room, and the phone rang. She had not been able to answer it previously, but this time there was an inner urging that gave her the motivation and strength, and she lifted the phone and answered.

On the other end was a friend who said, "I received the strongest impression possible that God is going to heal you. Now pray this prayer aloud after me."

And the friend prayed, "Lord, You said we could ask anything in Your name and You'd grant it. I claim that promise right now, and I praise Your name that *I am in this moment healed!*"

The woman repeated the prayer The power of God came upon her and she was healed, wonderfully and in a way no one could possibly dispute!

So what does this mean? That the woman who was healed had the proper amount of faith? It doesn't mean that to me, and she will tell you she didn't have "very much" faith when she prayed that prayer.

Here's what all this means to me: it means that *sometimes* the Master Computer-Operator Who sees all and knows all with an eternally loving eye says yes to this kind of praying.

The problem is that when this happens people get excited and overly zealous, and begin to assume they have finally "found the answer." "It works!" they exult, which really means, "We have found a way to mechanize God and make Him perform. We finally have God boxed in by His own promises and He can't get out of it!"

Mechanize God? Box in the Holy Spirit? Who is going to put a harness on the wind? Who will regiment a tornado? How can we put power steering on a hurricane?

We must say it again: God is not going to be formularized. You cannot say, "If we do A, B, and C, God will always do D." We may do ABC but sometimes He will do F or M or Z, if it is the *best* thing for those He loves. He will always do what *He* wants to do—you can count on that!

Also we must repeat that sometimes the most cutting, unkind thing one Christian can say to another is, "You must not have had enough faith" or even to ourselves, "Oh, if only I had had more faith."

Faith does not come in pounds and ounces to be parceled and weighed upon God's scales. Our study of the miracles of Jesus showed us that *sometimes* great faith seemed to be the key, but not *always*. Sometimes there was little faith or none at all. When will we ever finally learn that God will be God, and He will not be manipulated by us?

All this now leads us quite naturally to deal with a question which is a blood cousin to the one we have just discussed.

Will God give us anything we want?

The Bible *seems* to say He will. Our experience has been that He won't, so where is the discrepancy?

Here are the four chief Scriptures which allude to the above questions:

> Therefore, I tell you, whatever you ask in prayer, believe that you have received it, and it will be yours (Mark 11:24).

Whatever you ask in my name, I will do it, that the Father may be glorified in the Son (John 14:13).

You did not choose me, but I chose you and appointed you that you should go and bear fruit and that your fruit should abide; so that whatever you ask the Father in my name, he may give it to you (John 15:16).

So you have sorrow now, but I will see you again and your hearts will rejoice, and no one will take your joy from you. In that day you will ask nothing of me. Truly, truly, I say to you, if you ask anything of the Father, he will give it to you in my name. Hitherto you have asked nothing in my name; ask, and you will receive, that your joy may be full (John 16:22-24).

It is surely more than just coincidence that three of those four passages are all *conditional* promises. Jesus asks us, his disciples, to pray "in His name." How do you do something in the name of someone? Suppose you wanted to do something in the spirit (or the name) of Abraham Lincoln? Would you become an advocate of slavery? No, for that would be contrary to the spirit of the man and would dishonor his name.

Well then, the promise here is made to those *who pray in the spirit of Jesus Christ.* The promise is for those who do not violate His spirit in prayer. I somehow cannot imagine Jesus praying that a bald man would grow hair on his head. He could have, but what is important is that He didn't. Instead, He said His Father knew the number of hairs on our heads, and I presume if that number were zero God would know that too (and be aware of the best thing to do about it).

What is praying in the spirit of Jesus? Well, He said it was His greatest joy ("my meat," He called it) to do the will of His Father. His spirit, or attitude, was that there are only two ways to live in this world—God's way and God's way!

Surely our God is too wise to be a Santa Claus or a big man with a book full of blank checks. Surely we don't see

Him as the great Present-giver in the sky! Not the God who hung bleeding and dying on Calvary *because we finally got what we wanted*!

I am so glad my earthly father loved me enough to sift out my requests and answer them on the basis of what he thought was best for me, and on the basis of his love for me, and his concern for my well-being. Surely I can trust my heavenly Father to be as wise and loving as my earthly father!

I do not know the final answer to this question any more than I know the final answers to all the other perplexing questions and problems of prayer. I know the Bible seems to say one thing and our experience another in this matter, but I know this is not irreconcilable with a good God, for I know *Him*.

You see, what most of us do is pick out first of all the answer we want. Then we seek a promise and try to fit it to the desired answer. After we have done all this, we go to God with our prearranged plan.

I was in a midwestern state conducting a prayer seminar when a very troubled young Christian lady came up to me and said she wanted to speak with me privately after the session.

She was terribly upset about the matter of her husband's salvation. She asked, "Are you familiar with the verse which says if two of you agree on something and ask God, it will be done?"

I said, "Yes, I know that verse." This is the verse to which she referred:

> . . . if two of you agree on earth about anything they ask, it will be done for them by my Father in heaven (Matt. 18:19).

She said, "Well, I read that, so I called a friend over to my house. We read it, got on our knees, and prayed for the salvation of my husband. That's been six months ago and not a thing has happened!"

I told her what I believe about praying for the salvation of another. I told of a woman whose husband received Christ and afterwards she told me she had prayed for her husband's salvation every day for forty years! I told her God was true and faithful, but it seems that in every promise made in the Bible, printed or not, He has reserved the right to be God in all things, and to always answer on the basis of His love for us. I told her that even though sometimes it *seems* that God has not kept His Word, if we know Him we know He is trustworthy. I do not believe one can sing "Standing on the Promises" if he does not trust in the Promiser!

The Bible says of Abraham's wife, Sarah, after God promised her the impossible:

> . . . she considered him faithful who had promised (Heb. 11:11).

So we simply cannot select the answer we want, choose the promise, and then go to the Promiser saying, "Now You must produce what I want!"

Take a look at Abraham himself. When the contract was made between him and God, he was ninety-nine years old. God promised to lead him to a city. He was 175 years old when he died, so this means that for the next seventy-five years he wandered about with his family, his flocks, and his servants, looking for the promised city.

He never built a house, a permanent residence; he lived in tents as a sojourner, a temporary inhabitant for the rest of his life. He was old and tired; he must have longed for rest. He could have afforded a house, but still he wandered because he not only believed the promise—he *trusted* the Promiser!

I know there will come a day when Abraham walks the

shining parapets of heaven and overlooks the New Jerusalem and the Lord God will surely say, "There it is, Abraham, the city of God, and you are its father!"

Believe the promises but also trust the Promiser. Can you not do this? Have you found a better way than to let God be God and honor our faith out of the love that sees and knows all things both now and forever?

Is it a cop-out to say "Thy will be done"?

The same school of thought which urges you to ask anything, claim the promise, and celebrate the fact that it has been done, will tell you it is a cop-out to ask and then temper your request with "if it be Thy will."

To some, this is an indication that deep down there lies a doubt that God will perform, that it shows a lack of faith. Therefore, they say, one should never pray and include "if it be Thy will."

Once more, what we believe about prayer reveals the kind of God we believe in. Therefore, if I think it shows a lack of faith to say "if it be Thy will," this will be an indication that I believe in a God who (a) responds favorably when the "right" words are said, and unfavorably if the "wrong" words are used, and (b) a God who *always* answers prayer on the basis of how much faith the pray-er has.

I do not believe it is a cop-out to use these words. If I do *not* use these words, immediately I have taken away every one of God's options. If He sees and knows a better way, I have insisted my way is the way He must pursue.

God knows the programming of mankind at a glance, not only for the present but for years and generations to come. For me to tell Him He must answer in *my* way seems insolence unthinkable. Rather than revealing a lack of faith, *to say "if it is Thy will" reveals implicit faith that God's way is ultimately the best.*

Finally, I do not think it a lack of faith to say "If it be Thy will" because of the instruction and example of our Savior. When he gave us the Lord's Prayer as our model, he placed specific emphasis on always praying that our Father's will be done right here, right now, even as it is being done in heaven.

And when under the low-hanging olive branches of Gethsemane our Lord Jesus knelt in agony in prayer, the redemption of mankind was at stake. When all God's hopes and dreams for our salvation hung tremulously upon His decision, Jesus laid it all back on the Father's will.

"If it be possible, remove this cup from Me," He said. In other words, "If there is some other way, if Your perfect will can devise another plan, then do it."

But then, His sweat falling like drops of blood to the ground, He cried, "Nevertheless, not My will but Thine be done." And when He said that, God's will *was* done! So when they led Him down the hill toward the city, there is a sense in which our redemption was already accomplished in the willingness to let God have His way.

Rome crucified His body, Jerusalem crucified His spirit, but He crucified His own will. God, the Master Computer-Operator, the eternal lover of our souls, was set free to do His perfect will so that once more we might be "at one" with Him.

How shall I handle the silences of God?

The most difficult facet of prayer is God's silences. To pray and to see no response is very taxing and frustrating to us. If only God would *say* no instead of letting His silence speak for Him! That is when our prayers seem "to go no higher than the ceiling." How often have I heard that, and how often have I experienced it.

Why does God sometimes just leave us dangling in silence when we pray? Obviously, I do not know all the answers to that, but there are *some* answers I can believe and in which my faith is bolstered.

116

Dealing With Questions You Always Wanted To Ask

The "hold" button on a telephone helps me here. Sometimes I believe God puts us on "hold." If He is at work in the world and in our circumstances and always working for good for those that love Him, sometimes He Himself must wait for the proper tide of circumstances to come about.

Here is just a very simple illustration. Suppose you live in St. Louis and your son John lives in Memphis, and you are praying for his salvation. Suppose also that there is only one other person in the world whom God can use to lead your son to Christ. There is only one other person—Joe—whose personality, views, and ability to relate will appeal to your son strongly enough to influence him in that decision. Joe lives in New York and is planning (unknown to you) to move to Memphis, but not until he has finished his job in New York, which will take a year. Obviously God must put you on "hold" until the circumstances evolve.

Admittedly this is an oversimplification, but it comforts me, for I earnestly believe Rom. 8:28 tells infinitely more about our God than we are ever really willing to believe! That in "all things" He is working together for our good, and that the interpersonal relationships involved in all this are only knowable and solvable by the Master Computer-Operator!

God's delays are not *always* denials! There are other reasons God sometimes puts us on hold, or exposes us to His silences. It comforts me deeply to hope and believe that sometimes His silences are really signs of approval. Sometimes He uses them as His very own means to give us a much deeper blessing than He could have otherwise if He rattled off quick answers and easy solutions.

Mrs. Charles E. Cowman, in that classical little devotional book *Streams In The Desert,** illustrates this beautifully in an old familiar story.

*Compiled by Mrs. Charles Cowman (Zondervan Publishing House: Grand Rapids, Michigan, 1965), p. 44. Our thanks to the author, whose address we were unable to locate.

A Christian dreamed she saw three others in prayer, and as they knelt the Lord Jesus drew near to them. As He came to the first of the three, He stopped and bent over her. He lingered a long time and spoke to her at quite some length, tenderly and lovingly.

He then came to the next, stopped for only a moment, touched her head, and went on.

He passed by the third woman so abruptly it almost appeared as if he were ignoring her. And the woman in her dream, watching in wonder, said, "How deeply and surely He must love the first one; He approved the second, but the third must have grieved His heart deeply, for He hardly gave her a passing glance!"

But then the Lord of Glory stood beside her and said to her, "O woman, you have wrongly interpreted what you saw. The first praying woman needs all the visible and tangible evidence I can give her of My love and sustaining strength; otherwise she would slip and fall from the narrow way."

He went on, "The second has stronger faith and deeper love, and I can trust her to trust Me however things go and whatever people do.

"But the third woman, whom I seemed not to notice, perhaps even to ignore, and to whom I neither spoke nor touched, has the deepest and most mature faith and love of all. I am training her for the highest and holiest service.

"She knows me so intimately and trusts me so utterly that she does not depend upon the outward signs of My voice, nor My touch, nor My spoken approval. She is not dismayed by any circumstances through which she passes. Even when logic and reason seem to dictate rebellion she is not swayed, for she knows beyond doubt that I am working for her here and for eternity to come. She is satisfied to wait for all explanations until later, for she knows whom she has believed!"

So if in the mystery of God's silences we can actually find

ourselves praising God for the silence, rejoicing that He has counted us worthy of enduring it, we will not question *why* He has placed us on "hold." For we know that in His own time He will answer the phone!

Now we have tried to meet head-on some of the questions people ask most. Perhaps they will be of help to many, and rebuff others, but upon this by now we all should be able to agree: that human prayer is a mighty weapon in God's arsenal in His warfare against sin and death. It is one of the "big guns" He uses when it is offered. With it he gives flight to the evil one and all his works, and gives answers far beyond what we even ask.

I believe it was William Sangster who said, "When we all get to heaven and see what prayer has done, we'll be embarrassed we didn't pray more!"

Chapter 10
Someone To Call On

DID YOU EVER have your pleasant little everyday world shattered by a few short, crisp, pointed sentences?

I have.

I have referred to this experience earlier, but now the time has come to bear witness to the marvelous miracle which prayer wrought in it all and how God worked exceeding good from evil circumstances.

The day it happened I walked out of the doctor's office hard up against reality, shocked and stunned.

He had just told me that tests had revealed a great aneurysm of the aortic artery in the abdomen. The aorta, the largest artery in the body, runs from the lower part of the heart along the spinal column down to the waist where it divides to supply blood to the legs. It is about the size of a small garden hose, and is the supplier for almost all the organs in the middle and lower portions of the body.

An aneurysm occurs when an artery is partially blocked by cholesterol desposits and the artery balloons out, like a weak spot in a tire. The doctor said to me, "You have three choices. First, you can do nothing and the balloon will burst and death will be almost instant. Second, you can do nothing and, if it doesn't burst, it will stop up completely and we'll have to amputate both your legs. Or third, you can have it fixed and you have a chance."

He called those choices!

He proposed to cut out the diseased portion of the artery and replace it with ten inches of Dacron artery, which he subsequently did, and now some of my waggish friends say I have finally become a full-fledged man of the cloth!

But for me the dilemma and the person had come together on that day when I walked out of his office. At this point all the game-playing stopped; all the unreal, the phony, the role-playing came to an end.

The questions came rolling through my mind in shocked disbelief that such a thing could happen to me. Did I have the resources necessary to meet this thing? Did I indeed believe in prayer? Either I did or I did not. Either God was my strength and my salvation or He was not. He was either my shepherd or He was not.

You see, when God set up the conditions of life He made it so that eventually the dilemma and the person come together. He does not arbitrarily sit up in the sky and point at this one and say, "It's time for you to have cancer," or "I decree you shall have a mongoloid child," or, "Now you shall have a terrible accident."

But in order to grant us a free will, among other things, He permits a freely operating universe (in which evil forces are also allowed to operate) and eventually all of us come squarely up against a set of circumstances which we, in our own human strength and resources, cannot handle. If it does not happen sooner, it will happen later, due to the X factor of biological death written in the earth. So nobody, but nobody, escapes this. Now it had happened to me.

I want to share some of the great lessons God taught me

during that one particular experience in regard to prayer and the plainly visible operation of the Holy Spirit within those circumstances, as well as the shadowy vistas of mystery that cover a God Who is the lover of our souls but Who will not become our puppet on a string.

Perhaps this one experience will point up the whole great arena of prayer better than a thousand hypotheses. Perhaps it will help us all to measure and evaluate the resources available in our own lives for the times when the dilemma and the person came together for us.

First of all, I learned that when the dilemma and the person come together, everybody needs a friend or a loved one who has hold of God—a wife, husband, father, mother, sister, brother, pastor, or friend. Everybody needs somebody in whom one has complete confidence that he knows God face to face and for sure. Then, even when one himself cannot pray, but can only fight the agony of the circumstance, there is power and strength that comes from the firm knowledge that the loved one is praying for him, and from the power released from that prayer.

After the surgery I was in the intensive care unit for a few days. Of course there was some relief from the pain in the drugs given, but their effects would wear off before it was time for the next injection. Then was when the pain became severest, and then was when loved ones would be allowed in for five minutes each hour.

I could not pray, but they came and prayed for me, my minister friends, my bishop, and others. But most precious of all were the brief visits of my dear wife, the mother of our children.

You see, I do not really know about the private lives of my minister friends or others; I only know them publicly. But I know about the private life of my wife, Martha. I have lived with her for over thirty years, and I know that if anybody has a personal relationship with Jesus Christ, it is she!

So she would come and stand by my bed, and I would sense her presence and open my eyes. Through the swirling torrents of pain I would see her face, and reach out and take her hand. I remember thinking later that as she held my hand in one of hers in prayer, she was holding the hand of Another, and there were nail scars in that hand. She would pray, and the strength to bear the pain would come boiling up and overflow and make me adequate.

Time and time again this happened, and time and time again the pain was transcended by the realized sustaining power of the Lord's presence. Everybody needs somebody who has hold of God. That is the first great lesson I learned.

I learned also that when the dilemma and the person come together, everybody needs the prayer power of others.

We *say* we believe in the power of prayer, but sometimes I wonder if we really do. We betray ourselves sometimes when we say, "Well, all we can do now is pray" as if that one last resource wasn't very much to have left. The surgeon, the antibiotics, the plasma—we've tried everything and all we have left now is prayer.

It is one thing to say we believe in intercessory prayer, and quite another to have experienced it. It was a bit over three weeks from the day I walked out of that doctor's office with the diagnosis until the actual surgery itself, so I had plenty of time to think. The surgeon had told it as it was, that this type of surgery was fairly high risk, and that there was danger from clotting and other things. Being pretty human I had some bad days.

I would crank up the old imagination and follow it, painting lurid pictures of what might happen, right on down to the funeral parlor. At first we decided I would just slip off to the hospital and not tell anybody until it was all over. How often people do that! But one day it seemed the Holy Spirit said to me, "You either believe in prayer or you don't. There are no two ways about it, so do you or don't you?"

That brought me out of it! Of course I did! Let me pause here to say that when Christian people quietly go off to the hospital without telling friends, they are cheating themselves out of the greatest resource God has to give them!

Such an action has its base origin in pride—pride which is reluctant to let the general public know there could possibly be anything wrong with us or our bodies. We are very well, thank you!

So once I decided I really *did* believe in the power of prayer, I began to write letters, make phone calls, spread the word by mouth; I would have taken a full-page ad in the *Kansas City Star* had I been able to afford it. I wanted all the help I could get!

Three mornings before the surgery I awoke to find it there; the tide of intercessory power was there and rising. I recognized it as the same awareness I had known on the platform with the Billy Graham team several years previously. All day long it rose up within me. Like the ship waiting in the locks at the Panama Canal, it bore me upwards and upwards until by evening I was buoyed and held up with a deep sense of calmness and all-rightness that nothing but prayer can give.

All across the country they were praying. A church in Florida called; from Kentucky, Tennessee, Texas, they called. A prayer group 250 strong sent word. Several churches near our home held prayer vigils. Literally hundreds of my beloved friends across this land were storming the gates of heaven with their love and prayers, and I knew full well what the song writer meant when he wrote:

> *Safe in the arms of Jesus,*
> *Safe on his gentle breast*
> *There by His love O'ershadowed*
> *Sweetly my soul shall rest.*

Everybody needs the prayer power of other people. That is why it is important to build up and enjoy Christian fellowship ahead of time. That is why it is vital to have a church or a group within a church in which there is deep, rich fellowship which calls forth earnest prayer and its power when one of the number is in need.

There was still another lesson I had to learn. I knew it all along, but I had to have its blessed confirmation. Everybody needs the divine presence!

When I was younger, friends used to ask me for my favorite Bible verse. I could not give them one, but now that I am older I have heard enough cries of pain and wept by enough graves that I have one. Here it is:

I will never fail you nor forsake you (Heb. 13:5).

I knew from waiting with others that the hours in the operating room can be an eternity to a patient's friends or relatives, so I asked one of my minister friends to wait with Martha. The surgery was scheduled for eight in the morning, and Martha and my friend were to come at seven so he could have prayer with us before the pre-operation tranquilizer took effect.

I awakened that morning with the mighty seas of intercessory prayer power holding me firm and secure. There was an elderly man in a bed next to mine. He was in pain, and we prayed together for a while. Then a nurse came to give me the injection, and I said to her, "I know the doctor has ordered you to do this, but I want you to know I don't need it! I was never any more tranquil in my life than I am right now."

She looked at me for a long moment and then said, "I believe you," but I guess she wasn't *that* impressed because she gave me the injection anyhow! Martha and my friend came in; he had a firm, confident prayer, and then came the man with the cart.

Someone To Call On

Martha kissed me, and the attendant wheeled me down the hall to a room where he prepared my body. Then he backed the cart out of the rather small room, and we began the trip down the hall to the operating room. We started rolling down the long hall and there was not a soul in it. The only sound was that of the wheels turning. I closed my eyes and whispered, "Father, into Thy hands I commit my spirit."

I kept my eyes closed a moment and then I opened them, and then it happened! *I saw the living, lovely form of the Lord Jesus Christ Himself!*

I saw Him!

He was moving down the hall with me, alongside that cart. I did not see in vivid, living color, but rather as Paul said, "through a glass darkly." But He was there; He was real, and I saw Him, and I *know* that I saw Him!

I closed my eyes again, and rivers and torrents and floods of indescribably deep peace and joy and assurance came coursing through my entire being as I sank into His loving care. I knew the *divine presence*. He had affirmed it!

Well, what happened? I am not a mystical person. Until then I had never in my life had even so much as a dream about Jesus. It was totally and completely unexpected. So what happened?

At once someone will say, "It was the drugs." What is there in us that causes us to think that if we can explain something God must not have been in it at all?

I do not personally believe it was the drugs; but even if it were, this does not take away the reality of it, nor does it mean God was not in it. If it *were* the drugs, this only says to me that we have a heavenly Father who loves us so very, very much, and who is so "touched by our infirmities" that He will use any medium He can to break through into our awareness and assure us that He has indeed not forsaken nor failed us!

What happened? Again, of course I do not know. But

what I *believe* happened is good enough for me at the present moment, for it brings me immeasurable comfort and gratitude.

It certainly did not happen because I said, "Father, into Thy hands I commit my spirit." I have said that before; in fact, I had said that days previous to that moment, and with as much completeness as I shall ever be able to do it, so it wasn't that. That might have been a *factor*.

But I believe that among those hundreds of people who were spending themselves in prayer for me that day there were those whose brokenness, whose selfless spending of themselves and whose concern for me, freed God to do what He otherwise could not have done. So He did the thing which He thought was best for me and which I needed most under the circumstances.

There is no one who knows more fully than I that this does not answer all the questions one might raise. Equally as marvelous things have happened when there was *no* intercessory prayer. But I do not wish or need to "explain" everything.

I have no wish to "explain" all that happened that day out there on that sandy little mountain shaped like death when God hung quivering and dying. I do not wish to "explain" what happened in that dark new tomb when sometime in the next three days there was a strange stirring and the grave clothes were neatly laid aside, when One came forth to put his arms around a lost humanity, alive forevermore and saying, "Because I live you too shall live."

I do not wish to "explain" prayer and death and dying, suffering, pain and joy, a sunset, a bride's laughter, or an ocean's angry roar.

I am a human person, and the most thrilling thing there could be for me at this point is to walk hand-in-hand the rest of the journey with Him who has breathed grace on my soul.

And then one day, when I am able to bear it, He will tell me more.